THE OWL
AND THE PUSSYCAT
WENT TO SEE...

A Musical Play

by
SHEILA RUSKIN
&
DAVID WOOD

Music & Lyrics by
DAVID WOOD

Based on the verses and stories of
EDWARD LEAR

SAMUEL   FRENCH

LONDON
NEW YORK TORONTO SYDNEY HOLLYWOOD

ISBN 0 573 05027 9

THE OWL AND THE PUSSYCAT WENT TO SEE . . .

First produced by the Worcester Repertory Company at the Swan Theatre, Worcester, on Boxing Day, 1968, with the following cast of characters:

Owl	Juan Moreno
Pussycat	Catherine Crutchley
The Dong with a Luminous Nose	Matthew Walters
The Quangle Wangle	Jack Tweddle
Mr Canary	Carl Davies
Mrs Canary	Emma Stevens
The Runcible Spoon	Sheila Ruskin
The Plum Pudding Flea	Michael Richmond
Professor Bosh	Alex Johnston
The Pig	Brian Hewlett
The Turkey	Brian Hewlett
Head Jumbly	Carl Davies
Jumbly Girl	Susan Dury
Jumbly Two	Emma Stevens
Jumbly Three	Angela Dale Collins
Birds	Susan Dury
	Angela Dale Collins

Directed by Mick Hughes

Designed by Mary Moore

Produced by W. S. G. Productions Limited at the Jeannetta Cochrane Theatre, London, on 17th December 1969, with the following cast of characters:

The Fishes	Beatrice Aston
	Christopher Biggins
	Johanna Cassidy
	Gavin Douglas
The Owl	Lionel Morton
The Pussycat	Carole Ann Ford
The Dong with a Luminous Nose	Monty James
The Quangle Wangle	Jack Tweddle
Mr Canary	Gavin Douglas
Mrs Canary	Johanna Cassidy
The Birds	Beatrice Aston
	Christopher Biggins
The Plum Pudding Flea	Allan Stirland
The Runcible Spoon	Sheila Ruskin
Professor Bosh	Roger Brierley
The Pig	Geoffrey Wright
The Head Jumbly	Christopher Biggins
The Jumbly Girl	Beatrice Aston
Jumblies	Johanna Cassidy
	Gavin Douglas
The Turkey	Geoffrey Wright

At the Piano: Malcolm Sircom

Directed by: David Wood

Designed by: Susie Caulcutt

The action of the play takes place at sea and in the Land where the Bong Trees grow

AUTHORS' NOTES

This edition is a prompt copy of the first London production, but we are certain that the play offers much scope for imaginative directors and actors; therefore the stage directions, design and lighting instructions given here should be by no means taken as the only way to make the play work, rather as a guide, based on one production which was successful.

For example, if the actor playing Owl can play the guitar, it might be effective for him to use it throughout the play, thus affecting the silhouette mimes. Indeed, the silhouette mimes, though extremely effective, were found impractical and therefore cut in an excellent production at the Phoenix Theatre, Leicester.

Costume designers may be helped by the original pictures of most of the characters to be found in most editions of Edward Lear. In the first production a cast of twelve was used. The Pig doubled the Turkey, and the four Jumblies also played Fishes, Birds and Mr and Mrs Canary.

Finally, *The Owl and the Pussycat Went to See* . . . was written for young audiences. Adults will enjoy it if their children are enjoying it. Therefore no "business" or "innuendo" should be put in purely for the adults, as unfortunately happens in many pantomimes. At the same time there should never be a hint of patronizing the children. The story, played for real, is what is important.

DAVID WOOD and SHEILA RUSKIN

CHARACTERS

Owl: Gentle, straightforward, lovable, warm, but somewhat slow-witted —he is often one step behind everyone else.

Pussycat: Direct, very practical, quick-witted; moves nimbly; should never be "coy or prissy".

Dong: Melancholic, lugubrious, sad; but not necessarily slow of speech.

Quangle Wangle: Bright, lively, sprightly; boundless energy and attack; very eccentric in personality and movement.

Plum Pudding Flea: The villain; should resemble both a flea and a plum pudding. Lear's character has only one leg; this may be impractical for the stage, but he must hop, not walk.

Runcible Spoon: Genteel, timid, spinsterish lady.

Professor Bosh: True blue gentleman; the last of the great Victorian amateurs. Enthusiastic, eccentric.

Pig: Fat, ponderous, greedy; his initial crossness should take the audience by surprise—pigs are usually expected to be friendly!

Jumblies: Strange, unpredictable, high-voiced, with green heads and blue hands; they should hardly ever stop moving.

Turkey: Elderly, well-meaning cleric; his absent-mindedness and addiction to Spoonerisms continually frustrate his good intentions.

[handwritten: For Chorus - in trees with moppet handpuppets.]

ACT I

SCENE 1

The set comprises a large, round, raked rostrum and behind it a curved rostrum which leads off stage on both sides; behind this a cyclorama follows the curve. This basic set is used for all the locations of the play, with simple pieces of scenery added when necessary. The use of different coloured lighting on the cyclorama helps to effect a change of scene or time.
Before the CURTAIN rises music is heard.

When the CURTAIN rises, four Fishes are discovered. The atmosphere is mysterious and magical. Owl and Pussycat are in position on the central rostrum, in semi-darkness.

No. 1   SONG: THE OWL AND THE PUSSYCAT   *[handwritten: Liz Helen Jonathan. Muppets.]*
Fishes The Owl,

Owl is picked up in the light; he moves in owl-like fashion, then freezes

    And the Pussycat

Pussycat moves in her light, then freezes   *[handwritten: All the female chorus.]*

    The Owl and the
    Pussycat

They come together, as the lighting increases

    Went to sea
    In a beautiful
    Pea green boat

Fishes bring on the boat from off stage. Owl and Pussycat board it

    They took some honey

One Fish brings on a large jar marked "honey" and hands it into the boat

    And plenty of money

Two Fishes bring on four bags of money and give them to Owl and Pussycat

    All wrapped up in a
    Five-pound note

Two Fishes carry on a huge five-pound note. All four Fishes hold the corners to allow Owl and Pussycat to throw the bags of money inside. The Fishes knot the opposite corners and hand it all back into the boat. Owl and Pussycat sit down

          The Owl looked up
          To the stars above
          And sang to a small guitar

Pussycat hands a guitar to Owl. The moon flies in. The Fishes lie down and rock gently, their fins suggesting the movement of the sea

Owl   O lovely Pussy,
          O Pussy my love,
          What a beautiful
          Pussy you are, you are, you are,
          What a beautiful pussy you are.

Pussycat (*speaks*) And you're so very elegant.
Owl (*speaks*) Am I really?
Pussycat Yes.

Owl and Pussycat laugh

Owl (*after a pause*) Why don't we get married?
Pussycat What?
Owl I love you so much—let's get married—now.
Pussycat Eh?
Owl This very minute.
Pussycat: But how can we?
Owl It's quite simple really. We ask a friendly vicar to . . .
Pussycat In the middle of the sea?
Owl Oh. Good point. No friendly vicars out here—only fish.
Pussycat Exactly. (*After a thinking pause*) Let's look for one!
Owl What, a fish?
Pussycat No, silly, a vicar.
Owl Yes! (*Doubtful*) Where?
Pussycat Anywhere.
Owl Then we'll keep going till we find somewhere.
Pussycat (*remembering*) And a ring—you have to give me a ring.
Owl But you're not on the telephone.
Pussycat A *wedding* ring.
Owl Yes, of course. A ring and someone to marry us. That's all we want.
Pussycat Let's hope we find them soon.
Owl Then you *will* marry me?
Pussycat Of course . . .

Owl and Pussycat wave and the boat sails on

Fishes (*singing as they start to exit*)

          They sailed away
          For a year and a day
          To the land where
          The Bong Trees grow.

    The Fishes exit

The boat stops, then the rope Bong Trees "grow" on either side. Owl and Pussycat stand up in the boat

Owl Well, we've arrived—somewhere.
Pussycat Looks like an island.
Owl Funny trees. Bet there are ghosts and beasties and things hiding them . . .
Pussycat Stop it.
Owl Just waiting to—pounce. (*He pounces on Pussycat*)
Pussycat (*taken by surprise*) Ah! Don't be silly. Let's go on land. We can try to find a vicar there.
Owl It's a bit dark to start vicar-hunting.
Pussycat I know, silly. We'll rest under the trees and start looking in the morning . . . (*Whispering*) Come on.

Pussycat climbs over, helped by Owl, and tiptoes through the "water" to the "dry" land

Ooh, it's cold; mind your tail feathers.

Owl climbs over and gets his feet wet

Owl Oooh! (*He joins Pussycat*)
Pussycat (*whispering*) Shhh. Pass me the luggage.
Owl (*whispering*) Right.

Owl goes back to the boat, getting his feet wet again

Pussycat It's ever so dark.
Owl (*struggling back with the honey*) I don't know why we had to bring this with us—it's so heavy.

Owl puts the honey down and returns to the boat to collect the money

Pussycat It won't be so heavy when we've eaten some.
Owl Here's the money. (*He hands it to her*)
Pussycat Good. Very useful. (*She puts the money down behind the honey-pot*)
Owl On an island? I doubt if they use money here. (*In his normal voice*) I say.
Pussycat (*frightened*) What?
Owl What are we whispering for?
Pussycat I don't know.
Owl There's no-one here to wake up!

They sit down back to back on the honey-pot, then look around

Pussycat It's ever so dark.
Owl Don't worry about the dark. Ah, Pussy (*He puts a wing round her*), at least we're on our own.

A moving beam of light appears from off stage

Just you and I, and there are so . . .

Pussycat (*seeing the beam of light and jumping up*) Aaah.

Owl (*not realizing*) Don't worry, Pussy; there's no need to be frightened of the dark.

Pussycat It's not that. (*Pointing*) Look.

Owl Really, Pussy, you are . . . (*He sees the beam of light*) Aaah. Oh, oh, I say. (*He jumps up, his wings starting to flap, but he tries to be brave*) Just your imagination.

Pussycat Then why are your wings flapping? You know your wings only flap when you're nervous.

Owl Well, I er—I'm not exactly nervous—just——

The noise of loud, bitter sobbing is heard from where the light is coming

(*Hearing the sobs*)—terrified! Let's move to the trees.

They start to move in opposite directions. Realizing they are thus separated they join hands and again start to go, but again in opposite directions. They come together again and becoming more confused as the sobs from off stage get louder, they cross over each other and end up separated again. Owl hides behind one set of Bong Trees, Pussycat behind the other

The Dong With A Luminous Nose enters

Dong (*sobbing*) Ah. Ah. Ah. It's no use. Ah. Ah. Ah. (*He sits on the honeypot*) I'll never find her, I'll never see her again.

Owl and Pussycat timidly approach the Dong, one large step for each sob

Ah. Ah. Ah.

Owl I say . . .

The Dong sobs very loudly, frightening Owl and Pussycat backwards. They regain confidence and approach again

Dong Ah. Ah. Ah.

Pussycat Excuse me . . .

The same business happens. Loud sob and retreat, then another try

Dong Ah. Ah. Ah.

Pussycat (*interrupting the Dong before the next loud sob*) Is there anything we can do for you?

Dong Yes.

Owl What?

Dong For a start you can get off my foot.

Owl (*doing so*) Oh. I'm sorry. Look, I'm Owl.

Pussycat And I'm Pussycat.

Dong How do you do? I'm Dong.

Owl and Pussycat look at him enquiringly

Owl Pardon?

Dong D.O.N.G. Dong.

Owl What's wrong, Dong?

Dong I've lost my Jumbly Girl.
Owl (*not sure of what the Dong means*) Oh dear.
Pussycat Where did you last see her?
Dong I can't remember. I've been looking for so long I've forgotten.
Owl But—sorry to sound stupid—but what is a Jumbly Girl?
Dong You've never heard of the Jumblies?
Pussycat No. You see we've only just arrived.
Dong Did you sail here?
Owl Yes.
Dong In a sieve?
Owl In a sieve?
Pussycat No.
Dong Aaah.

No. 2   SONG: THE SONG OF THE DONG   ~muppets~

Dong   The Jumblies came in a sieve, they did,
            Landing at eve near the Zemm'ry Fidd
            Where the oblong oysters grow;
            And I fell in love with a Jumbly Girl so fair
            With her sky-blue hands and her sea-green hair.

            O somewhere in valley or plain   *Dock cousin*
            Might I find my Jumbly Girl again;
            For ever I'll seek by lake and shore
            Till I find my Jumbly Girl once more.

            Such happy days while the Jumblies stayed,
            Dancing all night to the pipe I played;
            Till one day they sailed away.
            As the sieve grew smaller, my Jumbly Girl I saw
            As I waved good-bye, from the cruel shore.

All: O somewhere in valley or plain   *Jumbly girl oh Jumbly*
            Might I find my Jumbly Girl again; *girl*
            For ever I'll seek by lake and shore *will we find his*
            Till I find my Jumbly Girl once more. *Jumbly girl again?*

Dong   But because at night-time I could not see
            I gathered the bark of the Twangum Tree,
            From it wove a wondrous nose;   *All muppets*
            And all painted red, round my head with bandage tied
            It has holes all round and a lamp inside.

All   O somewhere in valley or plain
            Might I find my Jumbly Girl again;   *twice. everyone*
            For ever I'll seek by lake and shore
            Till I find my Jumbly Girl once more.

By the end of the song all three are seated on the honey-pot, the Dong in the middle and Owl and Pussycat perched on either side

Pussycat I'm sure you'll find her one day.

Dong Perhaps. (*He sighs*) You didn't by any fortubitous chance see a sieve at sea?

Owl No. Not even a boat. Only a few fish.

Dong Oh misery. But tell me, why have you come to this island?

Pussycat Well, we didn't intend to arrive here in particular. We just wanted to land anywhere and try to find a ring and somebody to marry us.

Dong Marry you . . . (*He starts to cry violently*)

Owl and Pussycat fall off the honey-pot. They get up and sit down again during the next speech

Oh, forgive me, but the mere mention of marriage makes me immeasurably morose and melancholic.

Owl Pardon?

Dong Sad.

Owl Oh, I see . . .

Pussycat strokes the Dong sympathetically; Owl, rather embarrassed, gives the Dong a hanky

Dong Most kind of you. How charming you are—and clearly so much in love—(*He cries again*)

Owl and Pussycat fall off the honey-pot once more

I'm so happy for you. (*He still cries*)

Pussycat (*getting up*) Can you help us at all?

Dong (*recovering*) I wish I could.

Pussycat Oh, please.

Owl (*getting up*) All we want is someone to ma . . .

Pussycat (*almost too late*) Shhhhh!

The Dong starts sobbing. Owl and Pussycat sit down again

Owl Oo—yes, sorry. Someone to help us to—you know.

Dong I'm sorry. It's impossible. I only have to hear the word "love"——

Owl and Pussycat anticipate the Dong's crying and raise themselves from the honey-pot to avoid falling off

—or "marriage"——

The business is repeated

—and I can't control myself. (*He sniffs and speaks through his tears*) And you two are so in love——(*He cries*)

Owl and Pussycat, taken by surprise, fall off the honey-pot

—that I should weep all the time (*he wrings out the Owl's hanky*) and use up all your handkerchiefs. (*He holds out his hand*)

Pussycat gives the Dong her handkerchief

Thank you. And what's more, my tears might put out the light in my nose and then I couldn't see to search for my Jumbly Girl.

Owl (*getting up and moving round to Pussycat*) It's all right. Don't upset yourself. We can start looking for someone to . . . in the morning. (*He helps Pussycat up*)

Pussycat Of course.

Owl and Pussycat begin to exit

Dong I'm so sorry I can't help. (*Thinks*) Wait. I think I know someone who can.

Owl and Pussycat run back to him

Pussycat Really?

Owl Who?

Dong I'm in lodgings at the foot of the Crumpetty Tree and my landlord is the knowledgeable Quangle Wangle. He knows everything about everything. He'll know someone who can ma . . . (*He starts sobbing*) I'll take you to him—(*sobbing louder*) with pleasure.

Pussycat Can we go now?

Owl Pussycat, it's a little late.

Dong (*rising*) I don't see why not. I'll guide you both by the light of my luminous nose.

Pussycat Is it far?

Dong We'll be there by morning.

The Dong exits

No. 2a

Music. Mime. Pussycat starts to exit, followed by Owl. She stops suddenly and Owl bumps into her. Pussycat points to the luggage. Owl goes back and picks up the money and starts to exit. Pussycat realizes that she is to carry the heavy honey-pot. Owl turns back waiting for her. Pussycat staggers towards him with the honey-pot and because he thinks she will drop it, Owl takes it, dropping the money in the process. Pussycat picks up the money and places it on top of the honey-pot, thus making it impossible for Owl to see where he is going. He staggers forward. Pussycat realizes he is going the wrong way, follows him and taps him on the shoulder. He turns, she hands him her tail and guides him off

Owl and Pussycat exit

The lights fade to a silhouette on the cyclorama, as the moon flies out and the boat exits

SCENE 2

Silhouette mime with music.
There is a stile in the centre of the back curved rostrum.

Owl, Pussycat and the Dong enter, the Dong carrying the honey-pot and Owl carrying the money. The Dong reaches the stile. He stops, and Owl and Pussycat bump into him concertina fashion. The Dong tries to cross over the stile but cannot because he is carrying the honey-pot. He hands it to Owl who has to hand the money to Pussycat in order to receive it. The Dong crosses safely. Owl goes to cross but cannot because he is carrying the honey-pot. He hands it to Pussycat who has to put the money down in order to receive it. Owl crosses safely and he and the Dong start to exit. They stop suddenly, realizing that Pussycat cannot climb over because she now has the honey-pot. They return to the stile and Owl takes the honey-pot from Pussycat. The Dong and Owl start to exit. Pussycat beckons and stops them—she needs help over the stile. Owl stretches an arm across but nearly drops the honey-pot. He tries again. And again. He then stretches out his leg which Pussycat uses to help her over the stile. The Dong, Owl and Pussycat start to exit. Pussycat taps Owl on the shoulder. All stop. Pussycat points to the money left on the other side of the stile. Owl shrugs his shoulders, hands the honey-pot to the Dong, and goes across the stile, picks up the money, and crosses back again. Dong, Pussycat and Owl exit

The lights fade to a Black-Out

SCENE 3

The Quangle Wangle's Hat Hotel.

Music. It is dawn. Mr and Mrs Canary and the other Birds change the set; they twitter gaily as they do so, and indeed throughout the scene they react to whatever happens with bird-like noises. They bring on a huge sombrero-type hat, underneath which, legs only visible, is the Quangle Wangle. They put it down below the central rostrum, the Quangle Wangle lying down underneath it. The Birds also bring on two flat Bong Trees and place one each side of the central rostrum. The Crumpetty Tree is flown in on to the central rostrum, and the stile is removed from the back rostrum. Finally, the sun flies in as the lighting increases. The Birds gather round the hat as the Dong, Owl and Pussycat enter. They stop and the Dong proudly points to the hat

Dong Here he is. The Quangle Wangle.

Owl and Pussycat, bewildered, bend to look under the hat

Ring the bell.

Pussycat goes to the hat and rings one of the bells on it. Quangle Wangle makes a loud snore, snort or whistle. At the same time one leg kicks forward. Pussycat surprised, rushes back to Owl and the Dong

Dong Try again.

Pussycat tentatively goes to the hat and rings a bell again. The same thing happens and again she rushes back to Owl and the Dong

Quangle Wangle (*waking up*) Aha! Customers, customers, customers. (*Stretching his legs*) Good morning, good morning, good morning, and a hearty welcome to the one and only Quangle Wangle's Hat Hotel. (*He orders*) Raise the roof.

The Birds, twittering as they do so, lift up the hat. The Quangle Wangle emerges. They put the hat down

Where are they? 'Morning, Dong. (*Seeing Owl and Pussycat*) Aha! Good day, good day, good day. An Owl and a Pussycat. Most distinguished. (*He claps*) Mr and Mrs Canary. Come and take our visitors' luggage.

Mr and Mrs Canary start to pick up the honey-pot and the money. Owl and Pussycat try to restrain them

Pussycat But, well, thank you, but you see . . .

Quangle Wangle I offer you a wide variety of accommodation, all of which is glorious, galloobrious and genteel—

Owl No, but I don't think you under . . .

Mr and Mrs Canary succeed in taking the luggage and return round the hat, placing the luggage by the Crumpetty Tree

Quangle Wangle —and available to you at all prices from the reasonable to the ridiculous. (*He goes to Owl and Pussycat and shakes hands with them*) How dee do, dee do, dee do?

Pussycat How do you do?

Owl Look, your hat is quite remarkable, but . . .

Quangle Wangle You like it? Splendid, splendid, splendid. Perhaps you'd like to know how I came to be an—(*relishing the word*) hotelier?

Owl (*under his breath*) Not really.

Pussycat I don't think we've got much choice.

All gather round the Quangle Wangle

No. 3 SONG: THE QUANGLE WANGLE'S HAT

Quangle Wangle At the foot of the Crumpetty Tree
For many years I sat,
But my face no-one ever could see
Because of the size of my Beaver hat.

And the longer I lived by the Crumpetty Tree,
The plainer than ever it seemed to me
That very few people came this way
And that life on the whole was far from gay
For the Quangle Wangle Quee.

Chorus (*including* **Owl** *and* **Pussycat**)
And the longer he lived by the Crumpetty Tree,
The plainer than ever it seemed to be
That very few people came this way
And that life on the whole was far from gay
For the Quangle Wangle Quee.

Quangle Wangle At the foot of the Crumpetty Tree
It soon became quite clear
That my hat was enveloping me
So much, no-one noticed that I was here.

Quangle Wangle *and* **Chorus**
Yes, the longer I/he lived by the Crumpetty Tree,
The plainer than ever it seemed to me/be
That very few people came this way
And that life on the whole was far from gay
For the Quangle Wangle Quee.

Quangle Wangle But one day to the Crumpetty Tree
Came Mr and Mrs Canary,
And they said

Mr *and* **Mrs Canary**
Did ever you see
Any spot so charmingly airy?
May we build a nest on your lovely hat?
Mr Quangle Wangle, grant us that.
Oh please let us come and build a nest
Of whatever material suits you best.

Quangle Wangle What could I do but answer yes?
Then besides, to the Crumpetty Tree
Came Stork and Duck and Grouse
And the Snail and the Bumble Bee;
They all said "your hat makes a lovely house."

Quangle Wangle *and* **Chorus**
And the Pobble who has no toes,
The Frog and Bisky Bat,
And the Dong with a luminous nose—
We all built our homes on the Quangle's hat.

So the longer I/he live/lives by the Crumpetty tree
The plainer than ever it comes to me/be
That now ev'rybody comes this way
And that life never was more bright and gay
For the Quangle Wangle Quee.

Quangle Wangle That's me!

At the end of the song the Birds return to their conversation on the hat

So how can you refuse?

Owl We'd love to stay here, but . . .

Quangle Wangle Splendidiness unlimited!

Pussycat But we can't . . . (*She looks towards the Dong, hoping he will explain*)

Quangle Wangle Friends of the Dong? For you a forty per cent reduction. (*Moving to the hat*) I can offer you two single rooms overlooking the Crumpetty Tree.

Birds Ooooh!

Quangle Wangle A double on the East West corner of the brim.

Birds Aaaah!

Quangle Wangle (*coming back to Owl and Pussycat*) And finest of all, for you my friends, la grande suite at the top of the crown.

Birds Hooray! (etc.)

Quangle Wangle (*indicating the crumpets hanging above the hat*) At no extra charge for breakfast each morning, fresh crumpets will be dropped from the Crumpetty Tree with butter and jam, of course. And to entertain you with music and dancing each evening—the renowned Hat Band.

Owl (*moving to the Quangle Wangle*) Well, your hospitality does all sound marvellous, but . . .

Quangle Wangle No buts . . .

Pussycat (*moving beside Owl*) But . . .

Quangle Wangle Naughty.

Pussycat (*desperately*) We've come here, because we want to . . .

Pussycat remembers, nudges Owl, pointing to the Dong. Owl whispers to the Quangle Wangle

Quangle Wangle (*loudly*) Oh, you want to be married.

The Birds react happily

Dong Married? (*He bursts into tears*)

Pussycat (*to the Quangle Wangle*) Now look what you've done.

Owl and Pussycat go to comfort the Dong. They help him up and lead him towards the Birds on the hat

Quangle Wangle Oh, come along, Dong, pull yourself together.

Dong I'm sorry, so sorry. (*He recovers slightly*)

Quangle Wangle After all, it's not every day we have a wedding.

B

Dong Wedding? (*He turns from the hat and starts weeping again*)

General sympathy for the Dong is interrupted by a fearful "boing-boing" noise which startles everybody. Panic. All scatter, running to hide; Dong behind a flat Bong Tree with one of the Birds, Mr and Mrs Canary in the brim of the hat or behind the crown, and the other Bird behind the Crumpetty Tree. Quangle Wangle is hidden behind the other flat Bong Tree, but seeing that Owl and Pussycat have been left bewildered in the centre, emerges and grabs them in the nick of time, taking them behind the Bong Tree.

The lighting fades a little. Enter the Plum Pudding Flea. Everybody hides, but peeps out to watch where the Plum Pudding Flea is going. The Plum Pudding Flea stops, barks ferociously and turns a 90 degree angle on the spot. He repeats this, thus facing up stage, whereupon all the heads hide again. Two more hops and he is facing front again. Satisfied there is nobody within eating range, he exits. The lights begin to return to normal and everybody emerges tentatively from hiding, but the Plum Pudding Flea suddenly returns R and all hide again as the lighting fades once more. He hops in a straight line and exits. The lighting returns to normal

Quangle Wangle (*first to emerge on to the central rostrum*) Spoo-oon, Spoo-oon. (*To Mr Canary, who is peeping from under the hat*) You, fetch the Runcible Spoon at once.

Mr Canary is frightened

Don't just stand there hopping, hopeless. *Fly!*

Mr Canary exits

(*Stepping off the rostrum*) All right, everyone, safe now.

All emerge. The Dong and the Birds return to the hat to recover from the frightening experience. Owl and Pussyeat come to the Quangle Wangle

Owl (*trying to be casual*) Er, um, what was that?

Quangle Wangle That was the terrible, notorious and thoroughly scroobious Plum Pudding Flea. The most loathsome Plum Pudding Flea that ever was. Beware, beware, beware. The Plum Pudding Flea is always ravenously hungry and will devour whole any living creature he can catch. Also his spots are contagious.

Dong (*emerging, leaving the Birds and coming to the Quangle Wangle*) They're catching too.

Quangle Wangle (*dramatically*) One touch and you will be paralyzed.

Dong Most ungalloobrious creature.

Owl Sounds it.

Pussycat But isn't he afraid of *anything*?

Quangle Wangle Ah yes.

Dong The Runcible Spoon.

Pussycat The Runcible Spoon?
Quangle Wangle Correct. Coming over now.
Owl But why should he be afraid of a spoon?
Dong Stands to reason. After all, how do you eat Plum Pudding?
Owl Quickly?
Quangle Wangle No, no, no. With what do you eat Plum Pudding?
Owl (*helpfully*) Custard?
Quangle Wangle No, no, no. A spoon, my friend, a spoon.
Dong And as the Runcible Spoon is the only spoon on the island——
Pussycat —he protects you from the Plum Pudding Flea.
Quangle Wangle *She*, my dear, *she*, the fearless Amazon of the cutlery canteen.
Dong The pugnaciable heroine of the Bong Trees.
Quangle Wangle The swashbucklingest swashbuckler.

Mr Canary enters, bringing the Runcible Spoon

Dong The most dangerous desperado.
Quangle Wangle Courageous in combat.

The Runcible Spoon approaches the Quangle Wangle tentatively, standing behind him and the Dong. Mr Canary returns to the hat

Dong Daringly defiant.
Runcible Spoon You sent for me?
Quangle Wangle Savage.
Dong A tigress.
Runcible Spoon (*tapping the Quangle Wangle*) I'm here.
Quangle Wangle Daredevil . . .

The Quangle Wangle turns. The Runcible Spoon jumps violently, screams, and faints into the Dong's arms. The Dong helps her up and she sniffs some smelling salts

Oh, there you are. Spoon, allow me to introduce you to the Owl and the Pussycat.
Runcible Spoon How do you do?
Owl She doesn't look very brave.
Quangle Wangle (*holding out his arm dramatically*) My dear fellow, you wait. One glimpse of the Plum Pudding Flea, and she becomes a tower of strength, a veritable fortress against . . .

The "boing-boing" noise of the Plum Pudding Flea is heard

Runcible Spoon The Plum Pudding Flea. (*She faints over the Quangle Wangle's extended right arm*)

Panic. The Birds scatter, their wings flapping; Mr and Mrs Canary end up hiding behind a flat Bong Tree, the other two Birds end up under the hat or behind the crown

Quangle Wangle (*business-like*) Come, come, Spoon. Hold her up, Dong.
(*To Owl and Pussycat*) Encouragement needed occasionally, you know.
Quick, behind me.

*The Dong holds up the Runcible Spoon, facing off for the Plum Pudding Flea
to see her. The Quangle Wangle crosses in front to behind the Dong, followed
by Owl and Pussycat, who stand behind the Quangle Wangle, thus forming a
line.*

*The Plum Pudding Flea enters ferociously, and stops when he sees the
Runcible Spoon. Both freeze with fear. The Plum Pudding Flea howls,
turns and hops off quickly*

Dong (*letting her go*) Well done, Spoon.

*The Runcible Spoon screams and faints backwards, knocking over the whole
line*

Quangle Wangle (*first to revive as they all begin to get up*) All clear, everybody.

The Birds reappear

No more trouble for a while. He's probably gone back to his pudding
basin to sulk.

Dong (*holding the Runcible Spoon's arm up*) And it's all thanks to the
Runcible Spoon.

General cheers

Runcible Spoon (*rather pleased, though a little embarrassed*) Thank you.

Quangle Wangle (*joining Owl and Pussycat*) Right, where were we? Ah
yes, you want to get married.

Dong Married?

*The Dong cries. The Runcible Spoon and the Birds comfort him, all going to
sit on the hat. During the following scene and song, the Dong falls asleep on
the hat*

Quangle Wangle Oh, control yourself, Dong. (*To Owl and Pussycat*) Well,
I think I can help you. What exactly do you need?

Pussycat A ring and someone to perform the ceremony.

Quangle Wangle It'll mean a journey of course. (*Struck by the idea*) How
nice. I'll come too. I can guide you.

Pussycat Thank you.

Quangle Wangle Now, let me think, let me think, let me think. Luggage.
Mr and Mrs Canary. Fetch the visitors' luggage.

Mr Canary ⎫
Mrs Canary ⎬ But we've only just taken it in.

Quangle Wangle Then bring it out again.

Mr and Mrs Canary collect the luggage from the Crumpetty Tree

What exactly are you taking?

Owl Some honey and plenty of money.

Pussycat Wrapped up in a five-pound note.

Quangle Wangle What more could we possibly need? I'll take nothing.

Owl I suppose the Runcible Spoon couldn't be persuaded to come too? Extra company, you know?

Pussycat And she could protect us from the Plum Pudding Flea——

Owl looks put out, his motives have been exposed

—just in case.

Quangle Wangle Quick thinking. Spoo-oon.

The Runcible Spoon comes from the hat

I'm sure she'll come.

The Runcible Spoon arrives and meets the Quangle Wangle

Spoon, how do you fancy a few happy days' holiday, touring around the island?

Runcible Spoon That sounds lovely

Quangle Wangle These two are—(*making sure the Dong cannot hear*) getting married.

Runcible Spoon How romantic. I can't wait. When do we depart?

Quangle Wangle This minute, and your main duty on the expedition will of course be to ward off the Plum Pudding Flea.

Runcible Spoon Oh dear.

Pussycat (*taking a pace towards the Quangle Wangle*) Please, Spoon.

Owl (*taking a pace towards Pussycat*) We'd love you to come.

Runcible Spoon Well, I . . .

Quangle Wangle And when our quest is accomplished, you can be bridesmaid to the happy couple. (*To Owl and Pussycat*) That's right, isn't it?

Owl Of course.

Pussycat Naturally.

Runcible Spoon (*after a pause*) All right. (*Coyly*) I've never been a bridesmaid before.

Mr and Mrs Canary arrive from the hat, and cross to the Quangle Wangle

Mr Canary ⎱
Mrs Canary ⎰ The Owl and the Pussycat's luggage, Quangle.

Mr and Mrs Canary put the luggage down

Quangle Wangle Splendid, splendid, splendid. And Mr and Mrs Canary, please will you look after the hotel for a few days? We're going away . . .

No. 4   SONG: OFF WE GO

All Off we go together
Through the bracken and the heather
Towards the hills of Chankly Bore;
Through the Torrible Zone, round the Trees of Soffsky Poffsky,

Walk and walk, then walk some more.

Owl, Pussycat *and* **Quangle Wangle**
The Owl and the Pussycat and the Quangle Wangle Quee
Off to find a ring are we;
Not forgetting the Runcible Spoon

Runcible Spoon
That's me!

Owl, Pussycat *and* **Quangle Wangle**
To protect us from the Plum Pudding Flea.

The Runcible Spoon faints

All From the Bay of Gurtle
Past the slipp'ry slopes of Myrtle
Across the vast Gromboolian Plain,
Up and down on the shores of the great Lake Pipple-Popple,
Let's all hope that it won't rain.

The Owl and the Pussycat and the Quangle and the Spoon,
Let's set off this afternoon,
In the hope that the wedding will be quite soon,
Then we'll dance by the light of the moon.

From the Gulf of Handel
To the coast of Coromandel
Where lives the Yonghy Bonghy Bo,
To the City of Tosh, in the land of Gramble-Blamble,
On our journey now let's go,
Let's go, let's go, let's go,
On our journey now let's go.

*Owl, Pussycat, the Quangle Wangle and the Runcible Spoon exit. The
Crumpetty Tree flies out*

The Birds lift up the hat, waking the Dong in the process

Dong (*waking*) Hey, where are they off to?
Mr Canary (*clearing away the hat*) They've gone to get married.

*The Birds exit, carrying the hat. To effect a later scene change, one Bird
can be left hiding behind a flat Bong Tree; this avoids a stagehand being
seen*

Dong Married? (*He burst into tears and sits on the central rostrum*) Oh
dear, oh dear. What a miserable day. I've done nothing but cry, I've
been up all night and I'm so tired——

The Plum Pudding Flea is heard approaching. The lights are fading slowly

—and now they've all gone off and left me, and there's the Plum Pudding
Flea hopping along this way, and I know I'll never find my Jum . . .

(*Realizing*) *The Plum Pudding Flea!* I must hide. (*He runs behind a flat Bong Tree, but suddenly emerges again and speaks to the audience*) Whatever happens, don't tell him which way they went. Please. (*He goes behind the Tree and watches nervously, hiding on whichever side of the Tree gives him most protection*)

The Plum Pudding Flea enters on the back rostrum and hops down to the central rostrum

Plum Pudding Flea Ha, ha, ha, ha, I saw them going off, oh yes I did. And what's more I intend to follow 'em. (*Audience participation should be encouraged here*) I'm extremely hungry, and a tasty meal of plump Owl, garnished with Pussycat and spiced with Quangle Wangle will be just the job, ha, ha, ha. (*He hops off the central rostrum*) I haven't had a proper feast for ages, and I'm getting so thin that I rattle around in my basin. So I'll eat 'em all, ha, ha, ha, ha. Off to get married are they? Soon put an end to that little plan. They're moony—(*sneering*) in love—ughhhh. Love is a Bad Thing. Anyway, their affair won't last much longer, ha, ha, ha. Right. Which way did they go? This way? That way? (*He asks the audience. They will probably give him the wrong way, assisted by Dong who indicates "Yes" or "No" by nodding or shaking his luminous nose from behind the flat Bongo Tree*) This way? Thank you.

The Plum Pudding Flea starts hopping off. The lights begin to increase. The Dong pops out from behind the flat Bong Tree

Dong (*to the audience*) Thank you, we really fooled him that time.

Suddenly the Plum Pudding Flea returns. The lighting fades again. The Dong jumps back behind the flat Bong Tree

Plum Pudding Flea Wait a minute, you're all goody goodies, so I don't believe you. I'm going *that* way, ha, ha. (*He starts hopping off in the opposite direction but checks himself,*) Was that Runcible Spoon with them? She was? I'll have to watch out for her. But I'm so hungry I could tackle even her today—and use her to eat all the others with— ha, ha, ha . . .

The Plum Pudding Flea exits. The lighting increases

The Dong emerges from behind the Bong Tree, frightened, and steps down from the central rostrum

Dong Ohhh, how terrible. I must do something to save them. What can I do? Can you think of a way I might save them? (*Audience participation should be encouraged here*) Warn them, that's it. Get to them before the Plum Pudding Flea, and warn them. (*He starts to exit, then stops*) But it's very dangerous. I might get gobbled up on the way. (*To the audience*) Listen, if you were me, would you try to save them?

Audience Yes

Dong Even if you might get gobbled up on the way?

Audience Yes.

Dong You would really be brave and save them?

Audience Yes.

Dong Then so will I. (*He starts to exit, but suddenly the light in his luminous nose goes out*) Oh, no, my light's gone out now. (*He returns to the central rostrum and sits*) It's one thing on top of another; it's all that weeping I've been doing. I'm completely circumflumigated without my light; it's all the Quangle Wangle's fault for mentioning you know what . . . (*He moans to himself as he tries to mend his nose*)

Meanwhile Professor Bosh enters on back rostrum, carrying a huge net, magnifying glass, umbrella, etc., attached to his person. He notices the Dong. He looks delighted and advances warily. The Dong doesn't see him coming. The audience may shout "Look out". At last Professor Bosh catches the Dong in the net

Professor Bosh Got one at last. (*He checks excitedly in his book*)

Dong (*struggling*) Help, help. It's the Plum Pudding Flea. Don't eat me, please don't eat me. I wasn't *really* going to warn them. I know you are hungry, but I'm not very tasty, really I'm not, I'm tough, tough—ohhhhhh!

Professor Bosh (*lifting the net and looking underneath*) Oh, goshngolly, I say, I'm most awfully sorry, old man, my fault entirely. (*He removes the net and consoles the Dong, patting him on the head*) What a blunder. I do apologize most frightfully sincerely.

Dong (*recovering*) That's all right. Phew. I thought you were the Plum Pudding Flea, come to eat me up.

Professor Bosh What a coincidence! (*He sits beside the Dong*) I thought *you* were a Plum Pudding Flea. Jolly rare, you know. That's what I'm here for, you see, searching for a specimen for my private zoo. My card. (*He hands the Dong rather a large card*)

Dong Thank you. (*He reads*) Professor—Bosh?

Professor Bosh Bosh, yes.

Dong Illustrious scientist.

Professor Bosh Scientist.

Dong Botanist.

Professor Bosh Botanist.

Dong Gastronomical chef.

Professor Bosh Chef.

Dong And part-time gentleman explorer.

Professor Bosh Part-time gentleman explorer.

Dong And I'm the Dong.

Professor Bosh And I'm the Dong—I mean, (*he stands and formally offers his hand*) how do you do, Dong!

Dong (*impressed, stands and shakes his hand*) How do you do, sir!

Professor Bosh Listen, old man, have you actually *seen* a Plum Pudding. Flea?

Dong Oh, yes, often.

Professor Bosh Recently?

Dong A few minutes ago. (*Pointing*) He's hopping after my friends, the monster. (*Starting to exit*) I have to reach them first to warn them, before he eats them up for his dinner.

Professor Bosh (*joining the Dong*) Then there's no time to be lost. I say, old man, may I pop along too? I could perhaps—(*picking up his net and indicating it*)—be of some service to you.

Dong (*sadly*) Delighted, sir.

Professor Bosh Come on then. (*He crosses in front of the Dong who does not move*) What's the matter, old man?

Dong I can't guide you, sir. My nose is out of order.

Professor Bosh You can't smell the tracks, you mean?

Dong No. I won't be able to see in the dark. My light's gone out.

Professor Bosh Oh, you poor chap. Let's have a look at it. (*He leads the Dong back and sits him on the central rostrum; he inspects Dong's nose with his magnifying glass*) I'm rather good at noses. Mmm, yes. (*He brings out a stethoscope and listens in to the Dong's nose*) Say ninety-nine.

Dong Ahhh.

Professor Bosh Mmm. Something wrong there. Say Ah.

Dong Ninety-nine, ninety-nine.

Professor Bosh Dear me, yes. Let's see. I know. Stand up, old chap. Put your left leg in the air.

The Dong does so

Good. Right arm up.

The Dong lifts his arm with difficulty trying to balance on one leg

Not too far. That's it. Close your eyes. (*He brings out a wooden hammer, holds his stethoscope against the Dong's nose, and taps him lightly on the head*)

Dong Ow.

Professor Bosh And again. (*A second tap*)

Dong Ow.

Professor Bosh Third time lucky (*A third tap*)

The Dong's light goes on

Dong Ow.

Professor Bosh Open your eyes.

The Dong opens his eyes

How's that?

Dong (*delighted*) As good as new, sir. Thank you. Right then . . .

Professor Bosh Let's get going.

No. 5   SONG: OFF WE GO (*Reprise*)

Dong *and* **Professor Bosh**
>   Off we go together
>   Through the bracken and the heather
>   Towards the hills of Chankly Bcre;
>   Through the Torrible Zone, round the Trees of Soffsky Poffsky,
>   Walk and walk, then walk some more.
Dong The Owl and the Pussycat, I must warn immediately.
>   Danger lurks round ev'ry tree.
Professor Bosh
>   I'll come too, if I may, for I hope to see—
>   And to capture—the Plum Pudding Flea.

Both From the Gulf of Handel
>   To the Coast of Coromandel
>   Where lives the Yonghy Bonghy Bo,
>   To the City of Tosh in the land of
>   Gramble-Blamble,
>   On our journey now let's go,
>   Let's go, let's go, let's go,
>   On our journey now let's go.

Professor Bosh starts to exit in the wrong direction. The Dong stops him

Dong (*spoken*) Hey, Professor, (*indicating the opposite direction*) it's that way.
Professor Bosh (*spoken*) Goshngolly, yes.
Both (*sung*) On our journey now, let's go.

>   *The Dong and the Professor exit.*
>   *The lighting fades to a silhouette. The Bong Tree is carried off by the*
> *Bird who is hidden behind it*

SCENE 4

Silhouette mime with music   **No. 5a**
>   (1) *The characters enter and mime their journey across the back rostrum.*
>   *There is an imaginary patch of mud in the centre. The Quangle*
>   *Wangle is followed by the Runcible Spoon, then Owl carrying the honey*
>   *and Pussycat carrying the money. The Quangle Wangle notices the*
>   *patch of mud; he gestures to the others to stop—they do so, but so*
>   *suddenly that the line concertinas. The Quangle Wangle cheerfully*
>   *picks his way through the mud, shakes his feet the other side and*
>   *beckons to the Runcible Spoon to come. The Spoon shakes her head.*
>   *Business is repeated. The Quangle Wangle shakes his fists, recrosses*

mud and carries the Runcible Spoon, keeping stiff, over on his back. He lets her down and again shakes the mud off his feet. The Owl throws the honey-pot across the mud to the Quangle Wangle and makes his way through the mud using his wings to balance. Pussycat, carrying the money and holding her tail up, crosses easily and daintily. She shakes the mud off her feet and all four exit.

(2) The Plum Pudding Flea enters in pursuit. He hops easily and happily through the mud, shaking his fist to incite audience reaction.

(3) The Dong and Professor Bosh enter. The Dong crosses the mud in a successful, though wobbly, fashion. Then Professor Bosh slips over in it, hanging on to his huge net for support. Dong pulls him out, using the net. They exit

The lighting fades to Black-Out

Scene 5

Another part of the island.

Owl and Pussycat, tired, enter and stop in the centre of the stage

Pussycat Who'd have thought a ring would be so hard to find?
Owl Who'd have thought this island was so large? My wings are dropping off.
Pussycat And my paws.
Owl How much longer, I wonder?

The Quangle Wangle enters, full of life and spriteliness. As he speaks he crosses behind Owl and Pussycat, then back in front of them

Quangle Wangle My, my, my. What a spendiferous trip. Having passed through the fantastical hills of Chankly Bore, let us now attack the vast galloobrious Gromboolian Plain.
Owl and **Pussycat** (to each other) Oh, no.

The Runcible Spoon enters, groaning with the weight of all the luggage

Runcible Spoon Ohhh. (She drops the luggage)

The Quangle Wangle jumps, then turns

Quangle Wangle On second thoughts perhaps we should have a rest first.

The Runcible Spoon takes the money off the honey-pot and places it down behind it

Owl Good idea, I'm sure Pussy could do with a rest. ⎱
Pussycat Good idea, I'm sure Owl could do with a rest. ⎰ *together*

They glare at each other, then smile thankfully. The Quangle Wangle crosses to the honey-pot and goes to sit on it at the same moment as the Runcible Spoon. He wins. She moans and uses her smelling salts again

Quangle Wangle Really, Spoon. For first class silver, you're extremely soft.
Runcible Spoon I'm sorry, Quangle, I am trying.
Quangle Wangle Yes, very trying.
Owl (*moving with Pussycat to the honey-pot*) Er, Quangle, if you cared to remove yourself, we could perhaps partake of some of our sustenance.
Quangle Wangle Pardon?
Owl (*pointing to the honey-pot*) Have some honey.
Quangle Wangle Oh, stupid me! (*He gets off*) Picnicketty time, everybody. (*He stands behind the honey-pot and opens it*)

They all gather round, eating honey in their various ways. Quangle Wangle is in the middle, with the Runcible Spoon to one side, Owl to the other, and Pussycat kneeling in front of Owl

Pussycat Mmm, scrumptious.
Owl It's the best quality I could get.
Quangle Wangle A feast fit for a beast. How are you doing, Spoon?
Runcible Spoon Extra sticky and quite delicious, thank you.
Quangle Wangle Eat up then. It'll give you extra strength to fight off the Plum Pudding Flea.
Runcible Spoon Oh dear, I don't think I fancy any more.

Pussycat yawns and stretches, Owl yawns discreetly

Pussycat Let's have a little sleep before we go on. (*She starts washing herself*)
Quangle Wangle (*going to the central rostrum and starting to lie down*) Good idea.
Owl (*joining Quangle Wangle on the central rostrum*) Just forty winks.
Runcible Spoon I'm sorry, but I think that would be most unwise. Oh dear.
Quangle Wangle Why?
Pussycat Aren't you tired?
Owl Little nap do you good.
Runcible Spoon You see—it's most embarrassing, but—I tend to sleep-walk.
Pussycat Sleepwalk?
Runcible Spoon Yes. I might wander off anywhere.
Owl You could always come back when you wake up.
Runcible Spoon (*on the verge of tears*) But on a strange part of the island, how would I know where I was?

Quangle Wangle Look here, don't cry; you're almost as bad as the Dong. (*He crosses to the Runcible Spoon*) You go to sleep and I'll stay awake and make sure you're all right.

Runcible Spoon Would you? Oh, thank you. I am rather tired.

The Quangle Wangle and Pussycat lead the Runcible Spoon on to the central rostrum. All settle down. Suddenly Pussycat sits up

Pussycat I suppose we're safe here?

Owl (*looking up from under his wing*) How do you mean?

Pussycat From the—(*whispers*)—Plum Pudding Flea.

Quangle Wangle Of course, of course. Anyway—(*yawning*)—I'm staying awake.

Pussycat Just in case. (*Coming down off the central rostrum; to the audience*) Will you watch out for us? (*Audience participation*) Will you? Thank you. If you see the Plum Pudding Flea, or even hear him, would you shout out and wake us up?

Owl (*coming off the central rostrum to join Pussycat*) That's a good idea. What we'd like you to shout is, "*Plum Pudding Flea.*" Can you do that? Oh, thank you. (*They start to move back to the central rostrum*) Wait a minute. I think we'd better have a practice first. We'll count up to three and then you shout, "*Plum Pudding Flea.*"

Owl and Pussycat conduct a rehearsal to get the audience going. At no point, however, should they come out of character

Pussycat That's marvellous, thank you.

Owl Thank you. Now we can get some shut-eye.

They return to the central rostrum and go to sleep

Quangle Wangle I don't know what you're worrying about. (*Beginning to yawn*) After all, I'm staying awake.

Pause. The Quangle Wangle blinks in a tired manner

Runcible Spoon (*sitting up suddenly*) Are you sure you'll stay awake?

Quangle Wangle Spoon, fret ye not.

The Runcible Spoon lies down again. There is a pause. The Quangle Wangle starts to nod off.

Runcible Spoon (*sitting up suddenly, as before*) Not nodding off, are you?

Quangle Wangle (*jumps*) Of course not. Go to sleep.

The Runcible Spoon lies down again. Pause. The Quangle Wangle starts to nod off. The Runcible Spoon, sitting up suddenly as before, starts to speak, but is cut off by the Quangle Wangle glaring at her. She settles again. Music, such as the Brahms Lullaby. The Quangle Wangle nods off and lies down, then suddenly wakes up and jumps. He smacks himself saying "naughty". The business is repeated. The third time he remains asleep. The Runcible Spoon after a pause, gets up and starts to sleepwalk, arms forward.

*The Runcible Spoon nearly falls off the rostrum, and continues around it
until she reaches the back and exits. The others, in spite of possible noise
from the audience, have remained sound asleep. The noise of the Plum
Pudding Flea approaching is heard. He enters, sees the honey-pot and the
money and then the three asleep, exults, is put off by the noise from the
audience and tries to quieten them. The Runcible Spoon enters, still sleep-
walking, and walks straight towards the Plum Pudding Flea. When she
gets very near, he sees her, screams and hops away to hide behind a
Bong Tree. The Runcible Spoon carries straight on to the central rostrum
and exits. Owl and Pussycat wake up. They rush forward off the central
rostrum and ask the audience what has happened. Have they seen the
Plum Pudding Flea? Where? The audience point. Eventually Owl and
Pussycat understand and move across the front. At the same time the
Plum Pudding Flea crosses behind them up stage. Owl and Pussycat
pretend that the audience is having them on because they cannot see the
Plum Pudding Flea. But now the audience is pointing to the Plum Pudding
Flea on the other side, so Owl and Pussycat move across the front. At the
same time the Plum Pudding Flea crosses behind them again. Owl and
Pussycat again cannot see the Plum Pudding Flea and pretend that the
audience is playing a joke on them. Meanwhile the Plum Pudding Flea
starts to advance greedily upon Owl and Pussycat. The Runcible Spoon
enters on the back rostrum, still sleep-walking. She arrives at the downstage edge of the central rostrum just in time to put her outstretched arms
around the Plum Pudding Flea's neck. He stops, turns, screams and hops
off in terror. Owl and Pussycat hear the scream, see the Plum Pudding
Flea exit and cross to watch him go. They do not notice the Runcible
Spoon leave the central rostrum and exit the other side*

Pussycat (*thinking of how they can protect themselves*) Spoon, Spoon!

*Owl and Pussycat rush to the central rostrum where Runcible Spoon was
sleeping*

Owl (*wings flapping*) Ooooh, Ooooh, Ooooh!
Pussycat Quick, wake up, Quangle. (*She shakes him*) Please wake up.
Quangle Wangle (*stretching and yawning*) Oh, goodness me. I must have
   dropped off. (*Seeing their agitation*) What is it?

Owl tries to speak but is unable to. His wings flap as he gestures furiously

Owl Oooh! Oooh!
Pussycat (*impatiently*) The Plum Pudding Flea is here.

Owl nods

Quangle Wangle Well, that's all right. One peep at the Runcible Spoon
   will scare him off.

*Owl and Pussycat gesture furiously, pointing to where the Runcible Spoon
was. The Quangle Wangle takes no notice, but carries on talking*

Honestly, what is the matter with you two? The whole point of bringing the Spoon on the trip was to scare off the Plum Pudding Flea, and
here you are, quaking and quivering because you think you've heard
him. All we do is wake the Spoon, and we're . . . (*He has indicated the
Runcible Spoon with his arm, and now notices there is nothing there.
Stopping abruptly*) She's gone. (*Standing up, raising his hands*) Ahhhhh!
Owl Exactly. (*Echoing Quangle Wangle's movement*) Ahhhhh!

The Quangle Wangle paces up and down nervously, followed closely by Owl

Pussycat It's your fault. You were going to stay awake. She must have
gone sleep-walking. She said she would.
Quangle Wangle (*prowling agitatedly*) Escape, escape, escape.
Owl Yes, but he'll follow us.
Quangle Wangle Mmm. And he must be very hungry by now.
Pussycat We must set a trap.
Quangle Wangle Yes, but how? A trap, a trap, a trap—something sticky,
sticky, sticky. What have we got that's sticky?

*With the least encouragement, the audience shout out "honey, honey";
the three pretend not to understand for a while*

Quangle Wangle (*eventually*) They're right! A honey trap.

No. 6   SONG: HONEY SONG

During the song, the honey-pot is opened and the honey is poured out

Quangle Wangle A honey trap.
Owl   A honey trap.
Pussycat   A honey trap.
All   A honey trap.

Pour, pour the honey
Pour, pour the honey,
For, for the honey
Is worth more than the money
We've got——
—in this situation—
Spread, spread the honey,
Licky, sticky and runny,
Won't it be funny—
Empty the honey-pot.

And the Plum Pudding Flea
Will never get free,
But in the honey trap, stuck will be.

Pour, pour the honey,
Pour, pour the honey,
For, for the honey
Is worth more than the money
We've got—
—in this situation—
Spread, spread the honey,
Licky, sticky and runny,
Won't it be funny—
Empty the honey-pot—
The lot—
Empty the honey-pot

The noise of the Plum Pudding Flea approaching is heard. All freeze

Quangle Wangle He's coming.

Pussycat points to the money and Owl rushes to collect it. Pussycat replaces the lid on the honey-pot and carries it behind the flat Bong Tree. The Quangle Wangle is looking off in the direction of the Plum Pudding Flea's noise, giggling with anticipation

I can't wait. Here he comes and he'll go slap, bang gedoing into that great slushy, mushy mess. Ha. Ha. Ha.

Pussycat (*arriving behind the flat Bong Tree*) Come on, Quangle.

Quangle Wangle Can't we stay and watch the stick-up?

Owl (*arriving behind the flat Bong Tree*) Come *on*, Quangle.

Quangle Wangle How will we know it's worked unless we have a little peepy-weepy? (*He looks off*) Aaah!!! He's coming.

The Quangle Wangle runs behind the flat Bong Tree. Three heads are just visible

The Plum Pudding Flea enters; he looks around cautiously, then hops down stage to talk to the audience

Plum Pudding Flea You rotten goody-goodies. You're all nasty, horrible, and scroobidoobious. It's all your fault. If you hadn't screamed out so voluminously and viciously, my dinner would be in there—(*pointing to his stomach*)—digesting. And instead I'm still ravishingly hungry. Yahhhh. Right. This time I'll get 'em—and watch it, you lot. If I don't find them soon, I'll come and gobble all of you up instead. Now whicn way did they go? (*Pointing towards the honey trap*) Did they go that way?

The three behind the tree nod their heads, miming "yes" to the audience, who follow their lead

Did they go this way?

The audience is led by the other three to say "no"
(*Pointing in the direction of the honey trap*) That way?

The audience—"yes"

   Are you sure?

The audience—"yes"

   Are you really, really sure?

The audience—" YES!"

   Ahahaha! They won't escape me much longer. (*He starts hopping towards the honey and gets stuck in it. He screams with confused rage*)

Owl, Pussycat and the Quangle Wangle tiptoe off, delighted

(*Struggling to free himself*) I'm stuck!

No. 7   SONG: I'M STUCK

                I'm stuck
                I'm stuck
                Just my flumpetty luck;
                I put
                My foot
                In this scroobious muck,
                And lor luvaduck—
                Now I'm stuck.

                I'll have my revenge
                On the lot of 'em;
                I'll chase them and race them,
                And get shot of 'em.
                They'll never forget me
                The way they upset me
                Just wait till I get me
                Revenge.

                I'm stuck
                I'm stuck
                Just my flumpetty luck;
                I put
                My foot
                In this scroobious muck,
                And lor luvaduck—
                Now I'm stuck—
                Revenge—
                I'm stuck—
                Revenge,
                I'm flumpetty scrumpetty,
                Up to my rumpetty
                (*growl of frustration*)
                Stuck!

   c

The lighting fades to a Black-Out, then comes up again, as the Dong and Professor Bosh enter. The Professor is rather hot and a little tired, and the Dong is carrying his net for him

Professor Bosh Oh my. I hope you haven't brought me on a wild Plum Pudding Flea chase. We've walked miles.

Dong They must be near here, Professor.

Professor Bosh I hope so.

Dong (*noticing the Plum Pudding Flea*) Professor, that veritably vicious looking monster over there is what you've been hunting for.

Professor Bosh (*looking through his telescope*) Goshngolly, Dong. Well spotted. Alpha plus. Just have a quick check. (*He consults his book*) Now, will it be under F for Flea or P for Plum Pudding? F for Flea, I should think.

Dong He appears to be resting.

The Plum Pudding Flea makes a loud sound of rage and tries to get free

Ooh. P'raps he's got indigestion.

Professor Bosh D, E, aha, F—Flatter floopy fish, Flamble-bamskin. (*He turns a page*) Flibbertigibbet, no, too far—here we are—Flea!

Dong Indigestion. Hey, you don't think he's indigesting my friends, do you?

Professor Bosh No, no. His spots would have turned bright red if he'd eaten them.

Dong Would they?

Professor Bosh (*reading*) Cool Superincumbent Cucumber Flea—Co-operative Cauliflower Flea—no. (*He turns a page*) Ponderous Pumpkin Flea?—no, too far—here we are. (*Raising his voice in delight*) Plum Pudding Flea.

Dong Shhh. He'll hear us.

Professor Bosh It's him, it's him. Look at the picture.

Dong I *know* it's him. I told you.

Professor Bosh Oh, yes, of course.

The Plum Pudding Flea makes another noise, and struggles hard to get one leg free

Dong (*handing Professor Bosh the net*) Hurry, Professor.

Professor Bosh Quite, quite. Now, where's my net?

Dong Your net?

Professor Bosh Yes, where is it?

Audience participation can be used here

Dong In your hand.

Professor Bosh In my hand. So it is. Thanks. Right. Here we go. Very, very quietly. (*They start advancing*) Not a sound. (*He trips up over the net*) Shhhh!

The Plum Pudding Flea makes a last gigantic effort and, helped by the clatter made by the net, gets himself free—in the nick of time, without realizing who is behind him

Plum Pudding Flea Aha.

The Plum Pudding Flea hops off

Dong Quick, Professor, *now!*

Professor Bosh *Charge.* (*He makes a war-cry noise*)

The Dong and Professor Bosh charge straight into the honey, and get stuck. The lighting fades as they struggle unsuccessfully to get out. In the Black-Out they exit

Music link   **No. 7a**

The Runcible Spoon enters downstage, sleep-walking. She nearly falls off the stage, turns around and walks up on to the central rostrum. Meanwhile the Pig, accompanied by Mr and Mrs Canary, enters, carrying the flat Bong Tree which he positions against the central rostrum. Mr and Mrs Canary carry on a cluster of boulders and position them on the central rostrum. The Pig goes behind them and crouches, so that his bottom appears to be part of the rocks and is indistinguishable from them. The only identifiable feature is his tail, which is very long and very curly, and sticks up in the air. The Runcible Spoon bumps into the rocks and exits on the back rostrum. Mr and Mrs Canary watch her exit, shrug their shoulders, and exit themselves

SCENE 6

Yet another part of the island

Owl, carrying the money, enters along the back rostrum. He is tired and, not noticing the Pig, goes to sit on him, facing off stage, thinking he is a rock. Just as he bends slightly, the tail tickles him. He leaps up, mystified

Owl (*jumping up*) Oooh. (*He sits again*) Oooh!

Pussycat enters along the back rostrum

Pussycat Owl. What are you doing?

Pussycat watches as Owl tries to sit again

Owl (*jumping up*) Oooh. Well, it's extraordinary. Every time I—(*he does it again*)—ooooh!

Pussycat (*moving across the back rostrum*) Stop playing. We've got to find the Spoon.

Quangle Wangle (*entering along the back rostrum*) What's the matter with you two?

Pussycat Owl is being a little stupid, that's all. (*She continues to look for the Runcible Spoon*)

Owl I'm not. It's just that every time I go to sit—(*he does it again*)—ooooh!

Quangle Wangle How strange. It is a prickle or a tickle?

Owl Pardon?

Quangle Wangle A prickle or a tickle?

Owl Well, I suppose it's more of a tickle than a prickle.

Quangle Wangle Good.

Owl Why?

Quangle Wangle You'd be in a pickle if it was a prickle.

Owl A prickle pickle? No, it's not that.

Quangle Wangle What?

Owl A prickle pickle.

Quangle Wangle What is it then?

Owl A lickle tickle.

Quangle Wangle A lickle tickle?

Owl Yes, whenever I start to sit . . . (*He tries to sit again and leaps up*) Ooooh!

Pussycat (*returning to the Quangle Wangle*) What on earth are you two on about?

Owl My lickle tickle.

Quangle Wangle His lickle tickle.

Pussycat What is it?

Quangle Wangle (*beckoning Pussycat very confidentially and whispering*) We don't know.

Pussycat (*whispering*) Why not?

Quangle Wangle We haven't looked yet.

Pussycat (*irritated*) Well, let's look then.

With three large steps they all make their way gingerly to the tickling spot, and turn to look together

Quangle Wangle (*seeing the Pig's tail*) Goodness!

Owl (*jumping*) What?

Quangle Wangle Gracious me.

Pussycat What is it?

Owl Do you suppose it's some kind of corkscrew?

Pussycat A pink corkscrew?

Suddenly there is a loud snore from the other end of the Pig. They all jump

Quangle Wangle A pink snoring corkscrew?

Owl A little unlikely, I admit.

Pussycat Let's investigate the other end.

*In a line they creep round to the Pig's head. After three steps, they hear
another snore and stop. They do not see the Pig's head which rises above the
boulders as he snores and then disappears from view once again. They take
another three steps; there is another snore and the Pig's head appears again,
this time staying in view and resting on top of the boulders. They stop and
this time see the Pig*

Quangle Wangle (*recognizing the Pig; very loudly*) Eureka, of course.
   This is no pink, snoring corkscrew. This, my friends, is a pink, snoring,
   recumbent piggy-wiggy.
Pussycat Really?
Owl So it was piggy-wiggy gimme lickle tickle?
Quangle Wangle That's right.
Pussycat Let's wake him up.
Owl Do you think he'd mind?
Pussycat Maybe he's seen the Runcible Spoon pass this way.

Pussycat goes to shake the Pig awake

Quangle Wangle Uh-huh. Naughty; allow me, please. Piggy-wigs can be
   dangerous if not woken in the correct manner. (*He taps the Pig sharply
   between the ears*) Knock, knock.

*The Pig snorts crossly and wakes up, lifting his head. He has a ring on the
end of his nose. Quangle Wangle does not notice this*

   Excuse me, Mr. Piggy-wig, sir. I wonder if you have by any chance seen
   the Runcible Spoon passing this way?
Pig (*furious*) Certainly not. (*He drops his head, then lifts it up again*)
   Now let me get some sleep. (*He goes to sleep immediately*)
Quangle Wangle (*noticing the ring*) Oh, galloobriousness unlimited. Do
   you see what I see?
Owl A surly pig.
Quangle Wangle No, no. Well, yes, yes. But what else?
Pussycat An over-curly tail.
Quangle Wangle No, no. Well, yes, yes. But look, look, look—a pinky,
   porky piggy-wiggy—with a ring on the end of his nose.
Pussycat A ring——
Quangle Wangle —on the end——
Owl —of his tail.
Quangle Wangle ⎫
Pussycat ⎬ No . . .
All A ring on the end of his nose.
Pussycat Do you think he'd let us have it?
Quangle Wangle I don't know. He seems a bit attached to it.
Owl We could buy it——
Pussycat —with our five-pound note.
Quangle Wangle Five pounds? For a piggy-wig's ring?
Pussycat That's all we have.

Quangle Wangle No, no, no. You misunderstand me. A shilling would be quite sufficient. Let me quangle-wangle this. (*He knocks again*) Knock, knock.

The Pig snorts crossly and wakes up

   Excuse me, Mr Piggy-wig, sir.
Pig Certainly not.
Quangle Wangle We just wondered . . .
Pig Certainly not.
Quangle Wangle My dear, kind fellow.
Pig Certainly not.
Quangle Wangle No, you're certainly not.
Pig Clear off.
Quangle Wangle All I want . . .
Pig Clear off.
Quangle Wangle Just let me speak.
Pig Just let me sleep.
Quangle Wangle Oooooh you crosspatchetty piggy-wig.
Pig I know I am. I can't help it.
Pussycat There's no need to be rude, Quangle. (*To the Pig; gently*) What's the matter, Mr Piggy-wig?
Pig (*getting up*) What is it to you?
Pussycat We're interested to help you.

The Pig comes from behind the boulders and walks off the central rostrum. The others follow him

Pig And you won't laugh at me?
Owl Of course not.
Pig (*to the Quangle Wangle*) What about you?
Quangle Wangle I won't laugh. I'm too offended. (*He turns his back on the Pig, looking off stage*)
Pig I'm sorry, but it's my tail.
Owl (*sympathetically*) Then tell us it.
Pig (*turning to the Owl*) What?
Owl Your tale. Tell us it. The whole story.
Pig No. My T.A.I.L. tail.

To emphasize important words the Pig bounces up and down. This makes his tail tickle the Quangle Wangle, who begins to react, giggling

Pussycat What about it?
Pig (*bouncing up and down*) Everybody laughs at it because it's so curly. And all the birds think it's a nice big juicy worm, and try to pull it out and eat it.
Owl You poor porker.
Pussycat No wonder you're so cross.

The Quangle Wangle cannot control himself any more and laughs very loudly

Pig (*turning crossly to the Quangle Wangle*) There you are. You said you wouldn't laugh. I shouldn't have trusted you.
Quangle Wangle I wasn't laughing at you. Your tail was tickling me.
Pig Huh.

The Quangle Wangle and the Pig turn outwards so that they are back to back again

(*Noticing what the Owl is*) And you. You're a bird, aren't you? You'll be having a good old peck the moment my back's turned.
Owl Oh, I say. That's most unfair. I've been most properly brought up.
Pig (*with a big bounce*) Huh.

The Quangle Wangle bursts out laughing again

(*Turning to him*) There you are, you're doing it again.
Quangle Wangle (*turning to the Pig*) I'm not. It's your tail. (*He moves away from the Pig a little*)
Pussycat Listen. Let me mend it for you. I'm sure I could.
Pig Nonsense. Nobody can. Don't think I haven't tried.
Pussycat Quangle, sit on Mr Piggy-wig to stop him moving.
Pig (*facing off stage*) Now look here . . .

The Pig is too late, the Quangle Wangle is already sitting astride him

Pussycat And, Owl. Stroke Mr Piggy-wig under the chin to calm him down.

Owl strokes the Pig under his chin

Pig (*furiously*) How dare you. I'm perfectly calm. This is outrageous. You're wasting my time—and yours. (*He starts to enjoy the stroking*) I shall never have a proper tail. I was born to suffer. How dare you. That's rather nice. (*He giggles*) Take your hands off me. Mmmmmm. Lovely. (*He relaxes*)
Owl All right, Pussy.
Pussycat (*taking hold of the Pig's tail*) One, two, three, pull. (*The tail ends up completely straight and very long*) There we are, Mr Piggy-wig.

The Quangle Wangle gets off the Pig. Owl stops stroking him. The Pig looks at his tail

Pig Oh, thank you very . . . (*Noticing it is straight, he becomes very angry*) What! It's worse than ever; straight as a poker and long as a beanstalk.
Pussycat I'm so sorry. Let's try again. Owl, Quangle.

Owl and the Quangle Wangle control the Pig as before

Pig Oh, no, not again. Leave me alone. (*Eventually he relaxes with the stroking as before*)
Pussycat Ready? One, two, three, twist. (*She gives the tail three curls*) There.

Owl Oh, well done, Pussy.

Quangle Wangle Remarkable, remarkable.

Pig What have you done?

Pussycat See for yourself.

Owl Very handsome.

Quangle Wangle The best tail I've seen for a long time.

Pig Really? (*He sees it*) You've done it! Thank you, thank you. How on earth can I repay you? I'll do anything, anything.

Quangle Wangle Then help us.

Pig Of course. How?

Quangle Wangle These two want to get married, and you know what they'll need to do that, don't you?

Pig A ring and a vicar?

Owl Exactly.

Pussycat Well?

Pig Well what?

Pussycat Will you——

Owl —help?

Pig (*moving forward a little*) But I can't. I'm not qualified to marry people. I was always too bad-tempered to become a vicar.

Quangle Wangle No, no, no. They want your ring.

Pig (*looking at his hands*) So sorry. I never wear one.

The others point to his nose

Pig Oh. That one. My ring. Mmm.

Quangle Wangle Well?

Pig It's asking rather a lot.

Pussycat You said you'd do anything.

Pig But it's got great sentimental value. I've had it all my life.

Owl We could pay you for it.

Pig How much? (*Excited*) Sixpence?

Pussycat Sixpence?

Quangle Wangle Sixpence? They'll give you a shilling. Won't you?

Owl ⎱
Pussycat ⎰ Yes, of course.

Owl runs back to the boulders and fetches a coin from the bags of money, then quickly returns

Pig A shilling? Done.

The Pig gives Pussycat the ring. Owl gives him the shilling from one of their money bags

Pig Thank you. (*He returns to the boulders*)

Pussycat Thank you. Look, it fits. (*She puts it on her wrist*)

Quangle Wangle (*taking the ring*) I'll take charge of it till the wedding. I've just thought. I shall have to be the best man. Excitement unlimited.

Owl moves away and starts sniffing, slightly flapping his wings, and occasionally hopping

Pussycat Don't cry. You should be happy. All we need now is someone to marry us.

Quangle Wangle I don't think he's crying. Owl, what is it?

Owl I do apologize. It's just that I'm particularly susceptible to bad weather. All birds are, you know. I can feel in my bones the approach of a very rough storm. Most uncomfortable.

There is a slight rumble of distant thunder

Just as I thought. We'll have to take shelter soon.

Music and sounds of the storm. The Birds enter in panic, and all the creatures run about in fright

No. 8   SONG: FROM THE STORM

Owl, Pussycat, Quangle Wangle, Pig *and the* **Birds**

A storm is threatening
We'll get soaking wet 'n' when
The lightning flashes
And the thunder crashes
We must hide
From the storm.

A storm is brewing, we
Must stop what we're doing, we
Run helter-skelter
To a place to shelter
From the storm
From the storm.

The blustering wind
Blows up from the shore;
The clouds start emptying
Their torrential store
Of rain
Again.

The sky is blacker, how
The thunder is cracking, now
A gale is blowing
Rivers overflowing
And our fear is growing
So we must be going
We must hide
From the storm
From the storm.

The noise of thunder and rain becomes more violent. All rush off to hide. Lightning.

CURTAIN

*are standing in sieve looking
about.*

*chattering all time +
moving*

ACT II

SCENE 1

On the sea.
*One flat Bong Tree is in position against the central rostrum. Music is heard
as the storm continues.*

As the CURTAIN *rises, the Jumblies enter in their sieve. During the musical
introduction to the song they whoop with excitement and delight. As they
sing they move slowly across the stage*

No. 9   SONG: THE JUMBLIES' SONG

Jumblies
> Far and few, far and few
> Are the lands where the Jumblies live;
> Our heads are green, and our hands are blue,
> And we went to sea in a sieve.

More noises of enjoyment and laughter as they are tossed by the waves

> And when the sieve turns round and round and round and round,
> And ev'ryone cries, "You'll all be drowned, be drowned,"
> Then we call aloud, "Our sieve ain't big,
> But we don't care a button, we don't care a fig,
> In a sieve we'll go to sea."

*They excitedly chatter to one another: "O Timballoo, isn't it fun, how happy
we are, we won't get our feet wet because we wear pinky paper round them;
I'm hungry, are you? Yes; but isn't this lovely, being tossed around,"* etc.

> Far and few, far and few
> Are the lands where the Jumblies live;
> Our heads are green, and our hands are blue,
> And we went to sea in a sieve.

> The water's quickly coming in, it's coming in,
> But round in our sieve we spin and spin and spin,
> Though the sky be dark, the voyage long,
> Yet we never can think we were foolish or wrong
> In a sieve to go to sea. *That*

*They chatter again, "O Timballoo, how wise we are, what a lovely storm, I'm
a bit hungry though, aha land ahoy, perhaps there is food there, prepare for
landing!", etc. During the next chorus they arrive and "land" on the island,
pushing the sieve off stage*

Far and few, far and few
Are the lands where the Jumblies live;
Our heads are green and our hands are blue,
And we went to sea in a sieve,
And we went to sea in a sieve,
And we went to sea in a sieve.

[handwritten: pushing sieve out of sight]

*During the last line of the song the Dong and Professor Bosh enter, in semi-
darkness, and take up the same positions they were in when they got stuck
in the honey. Ooohs of excitement and cries of "Jumbly, Jumbly, Jumbly,"
as the Jumblies explore the island. Suddenly they see the odd sight of the
Dong and Professor Bosh, clasped together, eyes closed, frightened by the
storm and keeping warm, still stuck in the honey. They crouch under the
Professor's umbrella, the Dong clutching the Professor's waist, and head
out to the audience; he has fainted. Seeing the "monster", the Jumblies
twitter uncertainly, a little frightened. They are intrigued further when
Professor Bosh without looking up, suddenly moans, opens his umbrella,
and speaks*

Professor Bosh Oooooh dear, oh dear. What frightful weather. Dong.
Dong. Oh dear, he's still unconscious. Poor old thing, fainted during
the storm.

The Jumblies react, mystified

[handwritten: LAND + TAKE BEARINGS TOWARDS PROF onto rock still speaking]

Jumbly 2 Did it speak?
Jumbly 3 Speak?
Head Jumbly Speak?
Jumbly Girl Speak?
Jumbly 3 What a funny monster.
Jumbly 2 Monster?
Jumbly Girl Monster?

*Professor Bosh hears the noise and prepares to open his eyes, not knowing
what is going on*

Head Jumbly Monster—monster?

The Jumblies giggle, and echo "monster, monster"

Professor Bosh (*opens eyes*) Ah. Goshngolly.

The Jumblies laugh

Who—er what on earth are you?

No reaction from the Jumblies

Me, Professor Bosh. You?

Jumblies (*echoing the word*) You—you—you—yoohoo!
Professor Bosh My card. (*He hands them a card*)

The Head Jumbly takes it and takes a bite from it. Jumbly 2 grabs it and takes a bite and so on down the line. Finally, Jumbly 3 stuffs it in his mouth, but doesn't like it and reacts accordingly

Goodness, what strange creatures.
Head Jumbly We are the Jumblies.
Jumbly 2 (*echoing*) Jumblies.
Jumbly 3 Jumblies.
Jumbly Girl Jumblies.

All the Jumblies giggle

Professor Bosh Jumblies, eh? Good. Well. Let me look you up in my book.
Jumblies (*echoing*) Look in book, book in look (*etc., etc., giggles*)
Professor Bosh (*fumbling for his book*) Now then. Jumbly.
Jumblies Jumbly, jumbly, jumbly (*etc. etc.*).
Professor Bosh With a G or a J?
Jumblies GG? JJ? JJ.
Professor Bosh J. Here we are. Juby Jube, Jumpetty Jellyfish, Jongling Juggernaut.

After each name the Jumblies shake their heads

—aha—Jumbly—
Jumblies Jumbly, jumbly, jumbly (*etc. etc.*).
Professor Bosh (*reading*) —"idiotic creatures of little brain——"

Noises of agreement from the Jumblies

—"fond of practical jokes, naughty nonsenses and nonsensical naughti-nesses."

The Jumblies make noises of agreement

Oh dear, oh dear. "They have green heads, blue hands, and a tendency to wrap their feet in pinky paper!"

As the Professor checks each fact, the Jumblies helpfully point out each feature

"Contented and friendly creatures if well fed, but will become silly hooligans when hungry."
Jumblies Mmmmmm, hungry, hungry (*etc. etc.*).
Professor Bosh Mmmmmm. Are you hungry now?
Jumblies Mmmmmmmmmm. Hungry, very (*etc.*).
Professor Bosh Oh dear.
Jumblies Wheeeeeee.

The Head Jumbly leans over, knocks the book out of Professor Bosh's hand; the Jumblies play a catching game with it. Professor Bosh remonstrates; finally the Head Jumbly tries to eat it, but he doesn't like the taste and throws it back to Professor Bosh, giggling

Professor Bosh Oh dear. The sooner you have some food the better. (*To himself, remembering his predicament*) Not that I can do much to help. (*To them*) What do you want?

Head Jumbly (*bringing out a vast, long scroll labelled Shopping List and reading*) A pound of rice, some cranberry tarts . . . forget scroll

The Head Jumbly throws one end of the scroll over his head, allowing it to unwind down his back for the others to read

Jumbly Girl (*reading*) A hive of silvery bees, some jackdaws——
Jumbly 2 A monkey with lollipop paws.
Professor Bosh (*horrified*) To eat?
Jumbly 2 Oh, no. For a pet.
Jumblies (*echoing*) Pet, pet, pet (*etc.*).
Jumbly 3 An Owl.
Professor Bosh Another pet?
Jumbly 3 Oh, no. To eat.
Jumblies To eat, eat, eat (*etc.*).
Head Jumbly Our favourite food is roast owl.
Professor Bosh Really, most interesting. I must note that down. (*He does so*) Roast owl. Jumblies' favourite food.
Jumblies Mmmmmmmmmmmm owly, owly (*etc.*).
Professor Bosh Anything else on your list?
Jumbly Girl Forty bottles of Ring-bo-bee, an endless supply of Stilton cheese . . .
Jumbly 2 And a useful cart.
Professor Bosh A useful cart?
Jumbly 3 Yes, to put everything in.
Professor Bosh I see. And what makes you think you'll find all those things here?
Head Jumbly (*with mysterious superiority, as he rolls up his scroll*) Aaaaah!
Jumblies (*echoing*) Aha, aha, aha (*etc.*).

The Dong begins to wake up

Head Jumbly We know we can, because one of us has been here before.

General giggles

Allow me to introduce our incredibly well-travelled and beautiful— Jumbly Girl.

The Jumbly Girl comes forward and the others twitter away in excitement, clapping merrily LET HER THROUGH + MOVE BACK

Professor Bosh How do you do, ma'am?

The Jumblies giggle. The Dong, now awake, but still in the same position, has heard the Head Jumbly's words

Dong The Jumbly Girl?
Jumbly Girl (*thinking she heard the Professor*) That's right.
Dong It can't be.
Jumbly Girl (*a bit cross*) Of course it can.
Professor Bosh (*to the Dong*) Shut up.
Jumbly Girl (*crosser*) How dare you.
Professor Bosh Oh dear. No. I wasn't talking to you.
Jumbly Girl Then who were you talking to?
Dong (*with a cry of recognition*) The Jumbly Girl!
Jumbly Girl To me. I thought so. How dare you.
Dong It's her.
Professor Bosh Shut up.
Dong At last.
Professor Bosh Shut up.
Jumbly Girl (*realizing*) What's this? One monster, two voices?

The Jumblies "mmmmm" inquiringly

Professor Bosh No, no. You see, I'm not a monster.

The Jumblies "mmmmm" disbelievingly

No, I'm two monsters.

The Jumblies "mmmmm" with fright

No. I mean. I'm two people—things. Oh dear.
Dong The Jumbly Girl has returned. (*He starts to separate himself from Professor Bosh, and stands up*)
Professor Bosh You see? Look.

The one "monster" has become two. The Jumblies squeal with frightened disbelief and run away, clinging on to each other and shaking with fear

I'm Professor Bosh.

There is no reaction

And this is my colleague, the Dong.

The Jumblies gasp

Jumbly Girl The Dong? (*She excitedly comes forward to see him*)
Dong Yes, yes.
Jumbly Girl (*looking at him*) Oh. No, it's not. The Dong I knew once never looked like that.
Dong Yes, he did.
Jumbly Girl No, he didn't. He was a very handsome Dong, with a noble face.

Dong That's me. I mean, I am me. I mean, I am the Dong. (*To the Audience*) Aren't I? You see, when you went away, I vowed to find you; and so that I could look for you by night as well as by day, I put this light on the end of my nose.

Jumbly Girl (*delighted*) Then it is you.

Dong Yes. Now I've found you I don't need the light any more. I'll take it off.

Jumbly Girl No. Keep it on. Then you'll never lose me again. You dear Dong. (*She starts to move closer to him*)

Jumblies Dong, Dong, aaah (*etc., romantic noises, followed by giggles*)

Dong (*remembering*) Don't come any nearer.

Jumbly Girl Why not?

Dong The Professor and I, are, I'm ashamed to admit, stuck in this honey.

Jumblies Honey, honey, mmm, yummy, yummy, honey for hungries (*etc.*)

They all dash in front of the Dong and the Professor and fall on their knees, ready to lick the honey

Head Jumbly It won't fill a starving Jumbly tumtum, but it's a start.

They make approving noises as they start to lick. The Dong gazes lovingly at the Jumbly Girl

Wait!

The Jumblies stop eating

I know. You help us to find all the things on our shopping list, and we'll lick you out of this mess.

Professor Bosh That seems a fair offer. Eh, Dong? (*He sees Dong gazing lovingly at the Jumbly Girl—at a honey distance—and is embarrassed*) Oh dear. Yes. Well. I'm sure he'll agree—love, you know. (*He coughs*)

Head Jumbly Every Jumbly ready?

Jumblies Mmmmmmmmmmmm!

Head Jumbly Jumbly Girl? Jumbly Girl?

Jumbly Girl (*hearing, reluctant to look away from the Dong*) Oh—yes, ready.

Head Jumbly Off we go then.

No. 10   SONG: HONEY SONG (*Reprise*)

Jumblies

Eat, eat the honey,
Eat, eat the honey,
Sweet, sweet the honey
Makes a rainy·day sunny
~~And gay~~
~~it's so yummy yummy~~

Lick, lick the honey,
Thicky, sticky and runny,
Isn't it funny
Licking the honey away. ~~Away~~

Jumblies, Dong *and* **Professor Bosh**
Eat, eat the honey,
Eat, eat the honey,
Sweet, sweet the honey
Makes a rainy day sunny
~~And gay~~
~~—it's so yummy yummy—~~
Lick, lick the honey,
Thicky, sticky and runny,
Isn't it funny
Licking the honey away,
Away,
Licking the honey away.

During the song the Jumblies lick the honey away, until the Professor and the Dong are freed. (Note: The "honey" material can be surreptitiously put inside the Professor's umbrella, if this is left on the ground beside him. During the song, one of the Jumblies can do this) The Dong and the Jumbly Girl greet each other. The Jumblies make contented noises, the Head Jumbly rolling on his back with pleasure D L (Downstage left)

Professor Bosh Splendid, splendid. Did you have a good feast?
Jumblies Mmmmmmmmm!
Professor Bosh Good. Well, let's be off, Dong. Dong.

The Dong takes no notice. He is staring into the Jumbly Girl's eyes

Oh dear. Dong. We must continue our quest for the Plum Pudding Flea. REACT

The Jumblies scream in horror and clump together. Professor Bosh jumps. The Dong and the Jumbly Girl do not take any notice CLUMP

Head Jumbly The P-p-p-plum P-p-p-pudding F-f-f-flea?
Professor Bosh Y-y-y-yes. (*Recovering*) Why, do you know him?
Head Jumbly Yes. He's a scroobidoobious villain.
Jumblies Mmmmmmmm.
Professor Bosh Yes. Well, it's frightfully tricky, old man. I'm trying to capture him, and the Dong—(*He tries again without success*) Dong! Oh dear—he was helping me find him, because the Plum Pudding Flea——

The Jumblies react frightened again

—is chasing his friends, the Owl and the Pussycat.
Head Jumbly Owl?
Jumblies (*hearing their favourite food mentioned, begin to chant and dance around menacingly*)

Owly, Owly, favourite fowly,
Roast Owly, favourite foody.

Owly, Owly, favourite fowly,
Roast Owly, favourite foody.
Hunt for Owly. Owly, for hungry Jumbly (*etc.*)
Roast Owly, Roast Owly (*etc*)

The Jumblies, except the Jumbly Girl, dash off to find the Owl

Professor Bosh Yes, but you see—oh dear, oh dear, goshnogolly how
dreadful. Dong, they're going to eat Owly—I mean Owl.

No reaction from Dong

Come on. Oh dear. (*Rushing off in pursuit*) I say, I say, come back,
you chaps, and play the game.

The Professor runs off, leaving the Dong and the Jumbly Girl on their own

No. 11 SONG: A SYLLABUB SEA

Dong *and* **Jumbly Girl**
All of a tremble-bemble
Now I see,
Today at last
The storm has passed,
And left us here
In the calm of a syllabub sea,
Of a syllabub sea,
Of a syllabub sea.

All of a sniffle-snuffle
Now I see,
When all seems wrong
A moony song
Spongetaneously
Makes us calm as a syllabub sea,
As a syllabub sea,
As a syllabub sea.

Dong (*looking round*) Hey, they've all gone. Come on.

*The Dong and the Jumbly Girl exit. The lighting fades to a Black-Out. The
flat Bong Tree is struck. The lighting fades up to silhouette*

D

SCENE 2

The characters again mime their way across the back rostrum.

(1) *The Quangle Wangle carrying the money, Owl with wings flapping, and Pussycat enter and are confronted by an imaginary thin narrow pole which has to be crossed. Quangle Wangle crosses slowly and deliberately, almost losing his balance in the centre. Owl flaps his wings and takes a run at it. Pussycat, holding up her tail, crosses easily. The Quangle Wangle and Owl shrug their shoulders in amazement. All exit*

(2) *The Plum Pudding Flea enters hopping in pursuit. Half-way across the pole he starts to shake his fist at the audience so violently that he nearly falls off. He regains his balance and exits after the others*

(3) *The Jumblies, chasing after Owl, help each other across in their own mad way*

(4) *Professor Bosh, chasing after the Jumblies, notices the hazard. Raises his automatic umbrella and treads gingerly across. Closes his umbrella and exits*

(5) *The Dong and the Jumbly Girl follow. She is frightened by the pole. He gives her a piggy back. They cross in wobbly fashion and exit*

(6) *The sleep-walking Runcible Spoon enters, going in the wrong direction. By sheer luck, she crosses safely and exits*

The lighting fades to a Black-Out. The Turkey's house is flown in and a barrel of water placed by the door. The two flat Bong Trees are put in position either side of the house

SCENE 3

Outside the Turkey's house

The Quangle Wangle enters carrying the money, with Pussycat

Quangle Wangle (*very excited*) Well, well, well. My dear friends. This is the end, the final chapter of this our fizzgiggious journey (*He puts the money down by the door*)

Pussycat At last . . .

Quangle Wangle And the deserved fulfilment of all your ambitions is at hand.

Pussycat We can be married?

Quangle Wangle Yes, beloved, we can. (*He kisses her*)

Pussycat Quangle!

Quangle Wangle I mean—you can. Oh, flippetty dee. I'm brimming over with unlimited happiness for you both. (*Remembering*) If only the Runcible Spoon was here I'd be even happier.

Pussycat (*sobered*) Oh, yes, poor Spoon, poor Spoon.

Owl enters, wrapped up in the five-pound note

Owl (*quietly*) Er—excuse me.

Quangle Wangle What is it?

Owl Well, I don't want to be awkward and I'm very grateful to you, Quangle, but I would be even more grateful if you could unwrap me now. I feel like a parcel.

Quangle Wangle Ah, but is it safe?

Owl Of course.

Quangle Wangle No more flappetty wings?

Owl No. They're quite still now.

Quangle Wangle They nearly gave me a black eye.

Owl The storm's over now.

Quangle Wangle Are you sure you won't get over-excited during the wedding?

Pussycat Don't tease him, Quangle. I'll unwrap you, dear Owl.

Pussycat goes to Owl and unwraps him, then folds up the five-pound note and holds it over her arm

Owl Thank you, Pussy. I'll be fine now.

Quangle Wangle Pray silence. Be prepared, for the moment has come for me to knock upon this illustrious door.

Owl What for?

Quangle Wangle What for? Why, to call forth my distant relation, the Turkey.

Pussycat The Turkey?

Owl (*disbelievingly*) A turkey your distant relation?

Quangle Wangle Well, we live a long way from each other.

Pussycat But why are we going to see the Turkey?

Quangle Wangle Why? Because he is qualified to marry you.

Owl and Pussycat meet down stage

Owl Marry us? Oh, I say.
Pussycat Marry us? Oh, Quangle, thank you. } *together*

The Quangle Wangle prepares to knock. Suddenly the noise of the Plum Pudding Flea is heard

Owl Oh, no. The Plum Pudding Flea again. (*His wings start to flap again*)

Pussycat We must hide.

Owl and Pussycat turn outwards. Owl runs in a semicircle to meet the Quangle Wangle. Pussycat runs in a semicircle to meet the Quangle Wangle on the other side

Quangle Wangle Oh, horrors, horrors. (*He turns and bumps into Owl*)

Owl and the Quangle Wangle scream

Pussycat Quick.

Quangle Wangle What? (*He turns and bumps into Pussycat*)

Pussycat and the Quangle Wangle scream

Pussycat Hide.
Owl Where? (*He turns and bumps into the Quangle Wangle*)

Owl and the Quangle Wangle scream

Quangle Wangle Anywhere.
Owl Over there.
Quangle Wangle Where? (*He turns and bumps into Owl*)

Owl and the Quangle Wangle scream

Pussycat Here

Owl and the Quangle Wangle turn and bump into Pussycat. All scream

Behind the five-pound note.
Owl Good idea.

They unfold the note, hold it up and hide behind it, Owl in the middle. Owl's wings flap through the note

Quangle Wangle Stop flapping, Owl.
Owl I'm not flapping—much.

The Plum Pudding Flea enters

Plum Pudding Flea (*to the audience*) Lost them again, I have, thanks to you rotten lot of goody-goodies leading me into all that honey. Honey of all things—all sweet and nice and yucky—ugh! I hate anything sweet and nice and yucky. Anyway, I warn you, when I do find them there's going to be trouble, big trouble; oh, yes, full revenge and no mercy after that little bit of trickery. And you'd better watch out, too, or . . . (*He notices the five-pound note; to the audience*) Is that a five-pound note? It belongs to them, doesn't it? Oh, yes, it does. They can't be far off then; I'll have a little decko round here.

The Plum Pudding Flea goes to look behind the five-pound note. As he moves round, the note moves ahead of him, so that he ends up doing a complete circle. As the note turns round revealing Owl, Pussycat and Quangle Wangle, they gesture to the audience not to let on that they are there

Plum Pudding Flea (*emerging*) Not there. Just my flumpetty luck. Better make certain.

The business is repeated, this time in the opposite direction

(*Emerging*) No. They *can't* be far off.

The Runcible Spoon enters, sleep-walking

(*Pointing off*) I'll try this direction. (*Starts to hop*) And you lot had better watch it, or . . . (*He sees the Runcible Spoon. Freezes for a few seconds*) Aaaaaaaaaah!

Terrified, the Plum Pudding Flea exits

The Quangle Wangle, Owl and Pussycat drop the note and run to the Runcible Spoon

Quangle Wangle Splendid. Splendid. Done it again, Spoon.
Pussycat Well done, Spoon. Thank you.
Owl You were right, Quangle; she's the bravest spoon I ever met.

They pat the Runcible Spoon heartily on the back, and she wakes up

Runcible Spoon (*yawning*) What funny dreams I've been having.
Quangle Wangle Felicitations unlimited, Spoon. Yes, as I said, Owl, when roused, a veritable fortress against . . .
Owl Rescued in the nick of time. Thank you, Spoon, thank you.
Runcible Spoon (*still yawning*) Very strange dreams. Oh, that's all right.
Pussycat (*to Owl*) Wait a minute.
Runcible Spoon (*realizing*) Thank you? What for?
Quangle Wangle For banishing the enemy.
Pussycat (*to Owl*) She was still asleep.
Quangle Wangle Face to face combat with the arch villain.
Owl (*to Pussycat*) So she wasn't very brave after all.
Runcible Spoon Who?
Quangle Wangle The Plum Pudding Flea.
Runcible Spoon Ohhh. (*She faints across Pussycat into Owl's arms; he stands her up again*)
Quangle Wangle Come along, Spoon. Pull yourself together. Bridesmaid time.

Owl, Pussycat and Runcible Spoon go to the Turkey's door, led into position by the Quangle Wangle, who then knocks at the door

Now, everyone, lower your heads in reverence for a real live vicar.

The Turkey enters

No. 12   SONG: THE TURKEY'S SONG

Turkey I am the learned Turkey, and
      Of me you may have heard;
      Generally recognized
      A very wise old bird,
All   A very wise old bird,
      The Turkey,
Turkey Gobble, gobble, gobble, gobble, gob, I am—
All   The Turkey,
Turkey Gobble, gobble, gobble, gobble, gob,
      I am—
All   The Turkey who lives on the hill,
      Gobble, gobble, gobble, gob, gobble, gobble,
      Gobble, gob, gobble, gobble, gobble, gob.

Turkey Most erudite of animals
With several degrees;
Handsome fan of feathers too
And very knobbly knees,
All And very knobbly knees,
The Turkey,
Turkey Gobble, gobble, gobble, gobble, gob,
All The learned Turkey,
Turkey Gobble, gobble, gobble, gobble, gob,
All The learned Turkey who lives on the hill,
Gobble, gobble, gobble, gob, gobble, gobble,
Gobble, gob, gobble, gobble, gobble, gob.
Turkey A gallinaceous Doctor of
Divinity that's me,
Funerals and christ'nings for
A reasonable fee,
All A reasonable fee,
The Turkey,
Gobble, gobble, gobble, gobble, gob,
The rev'rend Turkey,
Gobble, gobble, gobble, gobble, gob,
The rev'rend Turkey who lives on the hill,
Gobble, gobble, gobble, gob, gobble, gobble,
Gobble, gob, gobble, gobble, gobble, gob.

At the end of the song Owl, Pussycat and the Runcible Spoon move and chatter excitedly among themselves

Quangle Wangle Melodiousness unlimited, Vicar.
Turkey Charmed, I'm sure; glad you enjoyed it. Hallo, it's Quongle Wongle, isn't it?
Quangle Wangle Well, nearly, Vicar.
Turkey Quingle Wingle? Quongle Pingle? Quengle Pongle!
Quangle Wangle (*helping*) Qua—a—a—a.
Turkey Of course. Stupid of me. Wangle Quangle. Good to see you, Wangle. I trust you are in good wealth—er, health?
Quangle Wangle Splendiferously so.
Turkey Splendisous—splenfous—splendof—good. Is this a bocial or a susiness call?
Quangle Wangle Both bocial—I mean social—and business really, both.
Turkey Delightful. What's it to be? (*Walking in a small circle*) Catechism? Confirmation? Communion? Funeral? Baptism? Mattins? Evensong? Ordination? Consecration? Or getting rid of ghostie—Exorcism . . .
Quangle Wangle These two friends of mine want you to marry them.
Turkey But I'm married already. Anyway, I couldn't marry two at once. (*He whispers*) Bigamy, you know.
Quangle Wangle No, no, no. They want to *be* married.

The Turkey looks uncomprehendingly

To each other. Urgently.

Turkey Ah. A Wedding. Why didn't you say before? Silly Wangle Quingle.

Quangle Wangle Pray allow me to introduce Owl and Pussycat.

Pussycat, the Runcible Spoon and Owl line up to be introduced. The Turkey walks over to them

Turkey (*greeting Pussycat*) How do you do, Owl? (*Greeting Owl*) And welcome, Pussycat.

Owl No, I'm not Pussycat.

Turkey I beg your pardon. (*Greeting the Runcible Spoon*) How do you do, Pussycat. My, my, so you're the brushing blide—er—the blushing bride, beautiful, beautiful.

Runcible Spoon (*embarrassed*) No, I'm the bridesmaid.

Pussycat *I'm* Pussycat.

Turkey Of course, stupid of me. (*Greeting Pussycat*) Please forgive me, Owl, stupid, stupid.

The Turkey sharply turns his back on them, his tail feathers forcing Pussycat, Owl and the Runcible Spoon to recoil. All give up trying to introduce themselves

(*Turning back*) Tell me, how long have you been married?

Owl Eh?

Pussycat We want you to marry us.

Turkey Of course, stupid. (*He turns*)

They recoil again

When?

Owl As soon as would be convenient.

Quangle Wangle Now.

Turkey Now? (*He turns sharply to the Quangle Wangle*)

They recoil again

Oh. (*To the Quangle Wangle*) Wongle, have they a ring?

Quangle Wangle Yes, yes. (*Irritated*) And I'm the best man. Now, please hurry.

Turkey It's highly irregular. And I have haven't got my Bayer Prook—er —Prayer Book.

Pussycat Please.

They all group as for a wedding, organized by the Quangle Wangle. Owl and Pussycat kneel, facing up stage, the Turkey standing above them. The Quangle Wangle acts as best man. The Runcible Spoon takes out her handkerchief

Turkey All right. Here goes. (*He coughs*) Please place the baby in my arms, and we . . .·

Quangle Wangle It's a wedding, not a christening.

Turkey Pardon. (*He coughs again*) Dearly—er—dearly . . .

Quangle Wangle Beloved.
Turkey Pardon?
Quangle Wangle Beloved.
Turkey How dare you. Cheeky fellow.
Quangle Wangle That's how it goes.
Turkey Eh?
Quangle Wangle It goes, "Dearly beloved."
Turkey Of course. Er—dearly befumbled—dearly belump-ed—oh dear—really we-shove-it—oh—beery delivered—I'm sorry, I'm all feduddled—er, befuddled—duddidled—Oh, it's no good, I'll have to book it up in my look—er—look it up in my book. It's so long since I did a widding—er—wed a didding—oh dear—did a wedding, I mean. Wongle Quongle Pongle, you'd better come and help me get ready.

The Turkey exits through his door, muttering "dearly belumped", etc.

The Quangle Wangle follows him, shrugging his shoulders to the others

Quangle Wangle (*as he goes*) All right. We'll leave the joyful couple on their own for a while.

  The Quangle Wangle exits

The Runcible Spoon, oblivious to anything but the happy pair, gazes at them dreamily

  The Quangle Wangle returns

Pssssst. (*He beckons the Runcible Spoon*)

Runcible Spoon waves cheerily to the Quangle Wangle, then looks back at Owl and Pussycat

Pssssst. (*He points to Owl and Pussycat and beckons the Runcible Spoon away*)

Runcible Spoon waves at the Quangle Wangle again and continues to stare. The Quangle Wangle goes to the Runcible Spoon

Spoon, will you please stir yourself?

The Quangle Wangle drags the Runcible Spoon into the house, she apologetically nodding

Owl and Pussycat, still on their knees, turn and face each other

Pussycat He didn't seem too efficient.
Owl At least he's qualified to marry us.
Pussycat That's true. Do you think we'll really be married soon?
Owl I hope so, Pussy. And we're nearer it now than we ever have been.

No. 13   SONG: A SYLLABUB SEA (*Reprise*)

Owl *and* **Pussycat**   All of a tremble-bemble
Now I see,
Today at last
The storm has passed,
And let us here
In the calm of a syllabub sea,
Of a syllabub sea,
Of a syllabub sea.

Singing a happy mumbian
Melody
Our troubles gone
Our love lives on
Galloobriously
In the calm of a syllabub sea,
Of a syllabub sea,
Of a syllabub sea.

Owl and Pussycat turn to enter the Turkey's house

ENTER D.R
Be all right.

The Jumblies come in, chanting (unaccompanied)

Jumblies Owly, owly, favourite fowly,
Roast Owly, favourite foody.
Owly, owly, favourite fowly,
Roast Owly, favourite foody.
Head Jumbly (*seeing Owl*) Owly!
Jumbly 2 Owly!
Jumbly 3 Owly!

PUSH D.C.

Squealing with delight, they surround Owl, pushing Pussycat away

Pussycat Hey, who are you? What are you doing?
Owl I say, stop it.

Jumblies dance around Owl, chanting merrily

No. It tickles. Stop it. Stop prodding me. You can't eat me. Help . . .
(*Etc.*)
Pussycat Oh, no. This is terrible. (*She rushes to the Turkey's door and bangs on it*) Turkey! Turkey!

The Turkey enters dressed for the wedding in his surplice, and carrying his Prayer Book

Turkey Don't be impatient. We've found my little book, so we're all ready for the joyful ceremony.
Pussycat It's not that. Those awful creatures have caught Owl—and—and—(*almost in tears*)—want to roast him.

Turkey Yes, well, there's no need to worry about that, it . . . What? How monstrous. Ah—(*seeing the Jumblies*)—the Jumblies. The Jumblies have arrived.

Pussycat (*pushing the Turkey towards the Jumblies*) Stop them, please.

The Quangle Wangle and the Runcible Spoon enter from the house dressed for the wedding. The Quangle Wangle has a buttonhole, and the Runcible Spoon a bouquet

Turkey What's this nonsense? Let the Owl go . . . PUSH HIM BACK

The Jumblies push the Turkey. Pussycat pushes him back towards the Jumblies

Pussycat Please try again.

Turkey You can't eat him; he's about to be married . . .

The Jumblies push him away again. The Runcible Spoon goes to comfort Pussycat

Quangle Wangle (*rushing to catch the Turkey*) You naughty, naughty Jumblies. Behave yourselves.

The Jumblies' chanting gets louder and more business-like

Jumblies O was once a little owl
    Owly
    Prowly
    Howly
    Owly
    Browny fowly
    Tasty owly.
    O was once a little owl. (*Etc.*)

Turkey (*dashing into the house*) Leave it to me, I'll meach them some tanners, the rascals.

The Turkey exits

The Quangle Wangle goes to the Runcible Spoon and Pussycat; they mime a conversation, discussing how to rescue Owl. They have an idea. The Quangle Wangle and Pussycat pick up the five-pound note which is lying behind them. They hold up the note and advance stealthily. The Runcible Spoon stays where she is, looking helpful. As the Jumblies circle, they spin them one by one into the note, until they are wrapped in it. They continue to circle slowly in the note, their heads peeping over the top; they mumble softly to themselves. Owl escapes, flapping furiously, and goes to the Runcible Spoon

Owl (*still caught up in the rhythm*) Owly, owly, favourite fowly . . . (*Etc.*)

Runcible Spoon You poor creature. Smell my flowers. (*To the others*) This will revive him.

Owl smells them and sneezes violently

Set LS note scene organised

Quangle Wangle Better, old friend?

Owl Oh. Thank you, thank you. You saved my life. I only have one, you know. Pussy has nine.

Professor Bosh enters

Pussycat Only eight after that fright.

Owl, Pussycat, the Quangle Wangle and the Runcible Spoon continue to chat

Professor Bosh (*seeing the Jumblies in the note, still going round*) Good morning. (*Realizing*) Good heavens—a revolving five-pound note. I must make a note of that. (*He makes a note in his book*) Good morning. (*He sees the Quangle Wangle*) Ah. (*Still breathless*) Excuse me, old man. Have you by any fortuitous coincidence seen the Owl recently? I've run all the way to warn him—the Jumblies are . . .

Quangle Wangle (*stepping aside to reveal Owl*) The Owl, sir—flappetty but free . . .

The Turkey emerges from the house with a truncheon

Professor Bosh Oh, Mr Owl. I'm so pleased to see you alive—I . . .

Turkey I'll get you, you scoundrels. How dare you interrupt our ceremony?

The Turkey knocks out Professor Bosh who falls. The Runcible Spoon kneels down and during the following scene, with Professor Bosh's head on her lap, tries to revive him

Owl But he came to warn me . . .
Pussycat You've hit the wrong one . . .
Runcible Spoon Oh, oh dear, what has he done? } *together*
Quangle Wangle The Jumblies are over there . . .
Turkey Where, where? Ah!

The Turkey goes and taps each of the Jumblies, who are still revolving, lightly on the head. This stops them mumbling and revolving

Take that!
Jumbly 2 Timballoo!   *sink to floor*
Turkey And that!
Jumbly 3 Timballoo!
Turkey And that!
Head Jumbly Timballoo!

The Quangle Wangle stays near the Jumblies, keeping an eye on them

The Dong and the Jumbly Girl enter

Dong (*seeing the Professor lying unconscious; to the Jumbly Girl*) The Professor—prostrate. Come on.

They rush towards the Professor

Turkey (*seeing the Jumbly Girl*) Aha, another one. (*He approaches her, raising his truncheon*)

Dong (*stopping him*) Hey. Hold on. You potty parson.

Turkey Porry—er sardon—I got carried away—stupid.

Dong What on earth is going on here?

Runcible Spoon This unfortunate gentleman was accident-
ally . . .

Owl These extraordinary creatures . . . (*Etc.*)

Pussycat They wanted to roast poor Owl . . . (*Etc.*)   } *together*

Quangle Wangle Well, Dong, it seems the Jumblies have
returned.

Turkey A most unfortunate event has prevented the wedding . . . (*Etc.*)

The Turkey raises his truncheon for silence

Turkey Let me explain. These pwo teople—er two people, asked me to woo a dedding—er do a didding—er wed a dooding—oh dear.

Quangle Wangle (*to the Turkey*) Allow me. The Jumblies tried to——

Pussycat —roast poor Owl.

Quangle Wangle Yes, just as he and Pussycat were——

Turkey —about to be married.

Dong Married? (*He bursts into tears*)

Turkey I'm so sorry. I didn't mean to . . .

Quangle Wangle Control, Dong, control!

Dong Wait a minute. I don't need to weep any more.

Quangle Wangle What? No more tears at the mention of the unmention-
able?

Dong No. You see, at last I've found my Jumbly Girl again. (*He tests himself*) Love. (*He pauses for a reaction, then smiles*) Marriage. (*He starts to laugh*) Love. (*He laughs more*) Wedding. Ha. Ha. Ha. And it's all thanks to my Jumbly Girl.

Jumbly Girl I'm never going to go away again. (*To the Turkey*) And I'm so sorry about the other Jumblies. They must have been very hungry.

Turkey They were so naughty I had to hash them on the bed—er bash them on the head. They'll wake up soon.

The Jumbly Girl goes to the other Jumblies

Runcible Spoon (*still nursing the Professor*) What about this gentleman? I hope he wakes up soon—he *is* rather heavy.

Dong Spoon. I didn't see you there. Thank you for looking after my friend.

Runcible Spoon That's quite all right. But who is he?

Dong (*proudly*) My colleague, Professor Bosh. We were coming to warn you.

Quangle Wangle (*shaking Professor Bosh's umbrella*) How dee do dee do, Professor? (*To the Turkey*) Well, now we've all been introduced, on with the wedding.

Pussycat Now?
Turkey Why not? (*He opens his book*)

Owl and Pussycat begin to move towards the Turkey. Owl pulls back

Owl Oh, but—I say—perhaps the ceremony could be conducted—
(*pointing to the Jumblies*)—out of temptation's way.
Pussycat Yes. You can't expect Owl to relax with the Jumblies so near.
Quangle Wangle More troublifications—but wait, a bright idea twinkleth
in my mind. To celebrate this auspiciously awful ev . . .
Dong Awful? I thought it was rather pleasant.
Quangle Wangle Awe—full—full of awe, Dong—aweful event, which
hasn't happened yet, but which will do so anon.
Dong What's a non?
All Ssssssh!
Quangle Wangle It is fit, seeming and entirely undesirable that we should
have a wedding feast——

*The Jumblies wake up, hearing the word "feast". They squeal and murmur,
'Foodywoody, Feastyweasty', (etc.).*

Quangle Wangle (*shouting to make himself heard*) —to which everyone will
be invited——

The Jumblies squeal even more excitedly

—except the Jumblies——

The Jumblies react, disappointed

—unless they behave themselves, and leave poor Owl alone.
Jumbly Girl You will, won't you? There'll be lots of food there.
Head Jumbly Yes, yes, we promise to be good. Anything for foodywoody.
Jumblies (*joining in*) Foodywoody, mmmmm, feastyweasty (*etc.*).

Professor Bosh begins to wake up, rubbing his head

Quangle Wangle That's settled then. A wedding feast. I think the Jumblies
may be unwound now.

The Jumbly Girl unwinds them.

Professor Bosh Ohhhhh! My head, my head.
Turkey (*helping him up*) My dear sir. Apologies, apologies. An errible
terror—er, a terrible error. Yow do you who? I'm the Turkey.
Professor Bosh (*with difficulty*) Good day. I'm Professor Bosh: illustrious
scientist, botanist, gastronomical chef and part . . .
Quangle Wangle Chef?
Professor Bosh Yes.
Quangle Wangle Splendid, splendid, splendid. You can prepare the feast.
Professor Bosh The feast? Goshngolly. You mean you're all going to eat
that poor Owl, and I've got to cook him for you? Oh deary me, I don't
think . . .
Quangle Wangle No, no, no. The Owl, sir, is to be married.

The Dong roars with laughter. All laugh

Professor Bosh Married?

The Dong roars with laughter. All laugh.

Professor Bosh In that case I'd-be delighted. But I haven't prepared a
wedding feast for a long time.

Quangle Wangle Nor have I.

Professor Bosh Are you a chef, too?

Quangle Wangle I run a hotel.

Professor Bosh Then give me a hand. (*To all*) We'll prepare the finest wedding feast you've ever seen.

Professor Bosh and the Quangle Wangle exit into the Turkey's house

*During the song the characters bring on a table and set it with all the in-
gredients for the cookery scene that follows*

SONG: THE WEDDING FEAST

All Plenty for all—
Man, bird or beast,
At the wonderful, whopping wedding feast.

Roast
Spiders and chutney,
Jelly and mince;
Raspberry vinegar,
Quail and quince.

Plenty for all—
Man, bird or beast,
At the wonderful, whopping wedding feast.

Boiled
Pelican pie with
Turnips and tripe;
Oyster patties all
Juicy and ripe.

Plenty for all—
Man, bird or beast,
At the wonderful, whopping wedding feast.
A glass of periwinkle wine
With eggs and buttercups fried with fish
Sitting, waiting, yours and mine,
Ev'ry exciting exotic dish.

Cold
Camomile tea with
Mulberry jam;
Parrot pudding with
Custard and ham.

Plenty for all—
Man, bird or beast,
At the wonderful, whopping, wedding feast.

Everybody exits into the Turkey's house

No. 14   Scene 4

Still outside the Turkey's house.

*From the Turkey's house enter Professor Bosh, dressed in chef's uniform,
and the Quangle Wangle, dressed in assistant chef's uniform*

Professor Bosh (*going behind the table*) Come along then, Quangle.
We've got time to make some really special goodies for the Wedding
Feast.
Quangle Wangle Splendid, splendid, Professor. Goody goody goodies.
Professor Bosh Right. First things first. Wash hands. (*He looks for some
water*)

*The Quangle Wangle starts licking his hands. Professor Bosh walks over to
him*

No, no. Don't lick your hands.
Quangle Wangle Sorry, Professor. (*He starts licking Professor's hands*)
Professor Bosh No, no. Don't lick my hands either. Wash them. *Wash.*
There's some water over there. (*Pointing to the barrel beside the Turkey's
door*) Fetch some in a bowl. (*He returns behind the table*)
Quangle Wangle Certainly, Professor.

*The Quangle Wangle picks up a colander and fills it with water. It sprinkles
out as he crosses the stage to Professor Bosh*

Here you are.

Professor Bosh (*absently putting his hands in without looking—he is checking
ingredients, perhaps*) Thank you, Quangle. (*He can't feel any water*)
Quangle. Please. Some water.
Quangle Wangle Sorry, Professor. (*The same business is repeated*) Here
you are.

Professor Bosh (*turning round just in time to see water spurting out*) Quangle.
I said a bowl, not a colander—that has holes in it. Here. (*He gives him a bowl*)

Quangle Wangle Sorry, Professor.

The Quangle Wangle fills the bowl with water from the barrel, returns—staggering under the weight—finds no room for it on the table, so puts it on the ground in front of the table. The Professor is still busying himself

Professor Bosh Hurry up with the water, Quangle. There's no time to waste. What *are* you doing, Quangle? Hurry up. Quangle, where is the water? (*Walking round the table towards the Quangle Wangle, he steps in the bowl*) Aaaah! You idiot.

Quangle Wangle (*trying not to laugh*) I thought you were meant to be washing your hands, not your feet, Professor.

Professor Bosh (*returning behind the table*) Now come along, be helpful. Put the bowl here. (*He slaps one end of the table and clears a place*)

Quangle Wangle picks up the bowl and, as though it is very heavy, staggers about. Professor Bosh is still checking things on the table

(*Slapping the table more firmly and crossly*) Here. (*Slapping the table even more firmly and crossly*) Here!

The Quangle Wangle heaves the bowl up on to the table without Professor Bosh noticing

Here. (*His slapping hand goes in the water, splashing them both*) Aaaaah! Please. Try to be helpful. (*He washes his hands*) Fetch my cookery book. And don't drop it. It's most valuable.

Quangle Wangle Certainly, certainly, Professor, cookery book.

The Quangle Wangle exits through the door of the Turkey's house and returns with a large, heavy cookery book, just as Professor Bosh finishes washing his hands

Professor Bosh picks up the bowl of water, the Quangle Wangle drops the book on the table, making a very loud noise, and Professor Bosh jumps in such a way that the water from the bowl goes all over him

Trust you to make a big splash, Professor.

Professor Bosh (*drying himself*) Oh dear, oh dear. Quangle. Hand me the cookery book.

The Quangle Wangle does so, but it drops—on to Professor Bosh's foot

Ow!

Quangle Wangle Perhaps I ought to look after the cookery book, Professor.

Professor Bosh Oh, all right. But let me find the place. (*He takes it, opens it, and a large snake jumps out*) Aah!

Quangle Wangle It's a book worm.

Professor Bosh (*as he and the Quangle Wangle put the snake in a specimen box*) No, it isn't. It's one of my latest specimens, Quangle. For my private zoo. Where the Plum Pudding Flea will be, with any luck. (*Picking up the cookery book*) Now, follow this recipe.

Professor Bosh walks round the table towards the Quangle Wangle following closely behind him. Professor Bosh stops and the Quangle Wangle bumps into him

Professor Bosh (*jumping*) What are you doing, Quangle?
Quangle Wangle Following the recipe.
Professor Bosh No, no, no. Read the recipe. Read it. (*He hands the cookery book to the Quangle Wangle, and then returns behind the table*)
Quangle Wangle (*reading*) Amblongus Pie?
Professor Bosh That's right.
Quangle Wangle We can't make that.
Professor Bosh Why not?
Quangle Wangle We haven't got any fresh amblongusses.
Professor Bosh Mmmmmm. Good point. What about Gosky Patties?
Quangle Wangle Not for a wedding.
Professor Bosh Parrot Pudding with Lizard Lozenges?
Quangle Wangle I don't think Owl would fancy Parrot Pudding.
Professor Bosh Mmmmm. Good point. Might be one of his friends.
Quangle Wangle Got it, got it, got it.
Professor Bosh What, what, what?
Quangle Wangle An itch on the end of my nose.
Professor Bosh I don't know how to cook that.
Quangle Wangle No, no, no. A joke, Professor! (*Turning over the page*) How about Crumbobblious Cutlets?
Professor Bosh Of course. Crumbobblious cutlets. Excellent idea. You read it out.
Quangle Wangle Take several strips of beef . . .
Professor Bosh Easy. Here we are. (*He produces two large beef strips*)
Quangle Wangle Hold them up in the air in the left hand.

Professor Bosh does so, but they are clearly very smelly. He takes them to the Quangle Wangle

Professor Bosh You can do that.

The Quangle Wangle holds up the beef strips in his left hand

Quangle Wangle All right. Take a new clothes brush.
Professor Bosh (*returning behind the table*) Mmmm. Tricky. (*He produces a large broom from behind the table*) How about this?
Quangle Wangle That'll do. (*Reading*) Brush it up hastily.
Professor Bosh What does that mean?
Quangle Wangle Brush the beef strips up and down.

Professor Bosh does so, but the broom not only brushes the beef, but the Quangle Wangle's side as well. Every time it tickles his armpit the Quangle Wangle giggles and jumps

E

Quangle Wangle Ooh. It tickles. It tickles. (*Etc.*)

Professor Bosh That's enough. Now what?

Quangle Wangle (*reading*) Lay on the table.

Professor Bosh What?

Quangle Wangle Lay on the table.

Professor Bosh Are you sure?

Quangle Wangle That's what it says. There. Lay on the table.

Professor Bosh Very well. Though it seems awfully odd. (*He lies down on the table*) Now what?

Quangle Wangle Professor.

Professor Bosh Yes?

Quangle Wangle I think it means lay the beef on the table.

Professor Bosh Well, why didn't you say so? Making me look stupid. (*He gets up, takes the beef from the Quangle Wangle and lays it on the table*) Now what?

Quangle Wangle Take a soup ladle——

Professor Bosh Easy. (*He produces one, a large one*)

Quangle Wangle —and stir, going round and round rapidly and capriciously.

Professor Bosh Going round and round?

Quangle Wangle That's what it says.

Professor Bosh Oh, all right. (*He turns madly round and round on the spot, brandishing the ladle*)

Quangle Wangle Er, Professor—Professor.

Professor Bosh (*giddily stopping*) What? What?

Quangle Wangle Perhaps it means stir the beef round?

Professor Bosh Oh. Perhaps it does, yes. Good point, Quangle. Here goes. (*He stirs the meat on the table, until it falls off*) Oh dear, do you think it's all right?

Quangle Wangle (*picking up the beef and brushing the dirt off*) Yes, it's not too dirty. (*Reading*) Now, put it in a saucepan.

Professor Bosh Easy. (*He produces a large saucepan and puts the beef inside*) Now what?

Quangle Wangle Remove to a sunny place.

Professor Bosh Remove to a sunny place?

Quangle Wangle Yes.

Professor Bosh Right you are. (*He walks away*) I think there's some sun over there.

Quangle Wangle *With the beef,* Professor.

Professor Bosh Of course. (*He comes back, takes the saucepan and returns to his "sunny" place*) Now what?

Quangle Wangle Leave it there for about a week.

Professor Bosh Splendid. (*He realizes*) What?

Quangle Wangle (*joining Professor Bosh*) A week.

Professor Bosh We can't wait that long. Let's wait ten seconds instead.

Quangle Wangle ⎫
                ⎬ One, two, three . . .
Professor Bosh ⎭

Quangle Wangle What comes after three?

Professor Bosh Er—forty-eight? Perhaps not. Er . . .

Quangle Wangle (*indicating the audience*) Perhaps they know. Do you know what comes after three? *Four?* Would you count up to ten for us? Thank you. (*Together with the audience*) One, two, three, four, five, six, seven, eight, nine, *Ten.*

Professor Bosh That's splendid. Thank you. (*He returns behind the table, taking the saucepan with him*) What's next?

Quangle Wangle Add a few herring bones.

Professor Bosh Mmmmm! Tricky. Would these do? (*He produces two dog bones*)

Quangle Wangle Yes, throw them in.

The Professor does so

One hundred ants' eggs.

Professor Bosh Mmmm. Oh dear. Would one hen's egg do?

Quangle Wangle I expect so.

Professor Bosh breaks the egg into the saucepan and throws in both the yolk and the shell

Some oil of almonds.

Professor Bosh Oil of almonds?

Quangle Wangle Yes.

Professor Bosh What's almonds?

Quangle Wangle Almonds. Nuts.

Professor Bosh So it's oil of nuts?

Quangle Wangle Yes.

Professor Bosh Easy then. Nuts. (*He pours in some metal nuts*) Plus a few bolts. (*He pours in some bolts*) And now the oil. (*He pours in some oil from an oil-can*) Oil of nuts.

Quangle Wangle Then cover the whole . . .

Professor Bosh Hole? Which hole? Keyhole? Foxhole? Hole in the road?

Quangle Wangle No, no, no. Whole. The whole. Cover the whole.

Professor Bosh This one? (*He puts his hand over the Quangle Wangle's mouth*)

Quangle Wangle No. (*Freeing himself*) Cover the whole . . . cover the *lot* with four gallons of clarified crumbobblious sauce . . .

Professor Bosh Sauce. There it is. By you.

Quangle Wangle Ah yes. (*He picks up a large, squeezy-type container of sauce*)

Professor Bosh Right. Give it to me.

Quangle Wangle Pardon?

Professor Bosh Give it me.

Quangle Wangle (*looking at the sauce, and then at Professor Bosh, he asks the audience*) Shall I give it him? (*Audience participation business*) Shall I, eh?

Professor Bosh Stop playing, Quangle. Give it me.

Quangle Wangle squirts sauce all over the Professor

Aaaah! No. I meant give me the sauce. (*He takes it*) We have to put it on the beef. (*He squeezes it, but it squirts up all over the Quangle Wangle*) Oh dear. So sorry. There. (*He does it properly*) Now what?

Quangle Wangle (*reading*) Throw the whole lot out of the window.

Professor Bosh What?

Quangle Wangle Throw the whole lot out of the window—hang on—*or*, if you *really* want to eat it, put the lid on the saucepan——

Professor Bosh Yes. (*He does so*)

Quangle Wangle —and say Crumbobblious Cutlets three times, as loudly as possible.

Professor Bosh I can't speak very loudly.

Quangle Wangle Do you know, neither can I.

Professor Bosh I suppose everybody couldn't help, could they?

Quangle Wangle Why not?

They ask the audience to help. Then after a couple of practices, all shout as loudly as possible

All Crumbobblious Cutlets, Crumbobblious Cutlets, Crumbobblious Cutlets.

Professor Bosh (*looking inside the saucepan*) Goshngolly. Quangle, look.

They bring out an iced wedding cake

Professor Bosh
Quangle Wangle } A wedding cake.

No. 14a

Carrying the wedding cake, the Quangle Wangle and Professor Bosh exit to music, through the door of the Turkey's house
The music continues as Jumbly 2 and Jumbly 3 enter. They see the ingredients and utensils which remain from the cookery scene and begin to play with them. One stands on the broom as the other sweeps with it; one stands in the bowl and twists to and fro. Enter the Head Jumbly, who reacts crossly to the games. Using the word "Timballoo", he admonishes Jumbly 2 and Jumbly 3, whereupon Jumbly 2 makes sure all the ingredients and utensils are on the table, and pushes it off. Jumbly 3 tries to pull the bowl off the ground, but cannot do so because he is still standing in it. Eventually he falls over, kicking the bowl over his head. The Head Jumbly catches it and both exit.

The lights fade to a Black-Out

SCENE 5

Outside the Turkey's house after the wedding.

The music changes into a joyful voluntary as the lights come up and the wedding procession enters through the door. Owl and Pussycat enter first, arm in arm, followed by the Runcible Spoon, weeping quietly; she holds a bouquet of flowers in bridesmaid fashion and holds up Pussycat's tail as though it were a train; occasionally she uses it to dab her eyes. The Dong and the Jumbly Girl follow behind and the Turkey proudly takes up the rear. During the procession round, the Turkey's house flies out, revealing the Jumblies supervising two tables of food, on the central rostrum. As the music stops the Turkey goes on to the central rostrum to check that the Jumblies are behaving themselves and the procession becomes a wedding group. The Jumblies begin to hand round goblets of periwinkle wine

Come down either side of rostra.

Dong (*to Owl and Pussycat*) Congratulations. When I first met you I had no idea things would turn out so happily.

Owl Well, it's thanks to you we met Quangle Wangle and thanks to him we're married at last.

Pussycat Are you two going to be next?

Dong Yes, it's all arranged.

Jumbly Girl The Turkey has agreed to marry us whenever we like.

Turkey (*coming down from the central rostrum*) Indeed I have. I'm back in practice now, you know.

General laughter

Owl What about you, Spoon? When are you to be a bride?

Runcible Spoon Oh, Mr Owl—I—(*embarrassed*)—some day perhaps—I live in hope. (*She wipes away a tear*)

By now the Jumblies have finished handing round the goblets

Turkey There, there. (*Stepping forward a pace*) Now, let us all drink a toast of periwinkle wine to the happy couple. May all your problems be past. To you be ever love, happiness and peace . . .

Music. All group in readiness for the final song

All (*sing*) A meloobious sound . . .

"Boing-Boing"—the sound of the Plum Pudding Flea approaching—makes everybody stop singing and freeze with terror

Turkey Weapons, weapons. Fight the good fight. Find weapons at once.

The Turkey exits

There is general panic. Everyone rushes round terrified, especially the Jumblies CL

Pussycat Owl, what are we to do? (*Noticing the Runcible Spoon*) Spoon, it's up to you to save us.

Runcible Spoon (*swaying*) I'm sorry, The Plum—Pud-d-d-ding—Flea . . . (*She faints*)

Owl There goes our only defence, and we haven't anything to fight with.

Pussycat Wait a minute. What saved us from the Plum Pudding Flea last time?

Owl The honey.
Pussycat And what saved you from the Jumblies?
Owl The five-pound note.
Pussycat What have we got left?
Owl The bags of money.

Owl and Pussycat dash to the bags of money and begin to open them. By this time the others are hiding; the Dong and the Jumbly Girl are behind one table and Jumbly 2 is behind the other. The Head Jumbly and Jumbly 3 are hiding behind a flat Bong tree

Dong (*shaking very nervously*) I'll protect you, Jumbly Girl.
Jumbly Girl You're so brave, Dong. But why are you shaking?
Dong I'm so—excited.
Pussycat Take some money, everybody. (*She runs to the central rostrum and hands Jumbly 2 some money, then goes back to the Dong and the Jumbly Girl*) Every Jumbly too. (*She hands another bag to the Head Jumbly and Jumbly 3, behind the flat Bong Tree*) And hide. Wait for the word and then let him have it.

Pussycat runs to the other flat Bong Tree, where Owl is waiting for her with a bag of money. They hide. The "boing-boing" noises get louder. The Runcible Spoon is still lying in a faint

Jumbly Girl (*popping up from behind the table*) What about Spoon?
The Dong goes to fetch the Runcible Spoon, but sees the Plum Pudding Flea approaching

Dong No. Too late. (*He hides*)

The Plum Pudding Flea enters   look towards direct" of entrance

Plum Pudding Flea (*to the audience*) Aha, signs of a feast. Well, soon it's going to be *my* turn for a feast. I'm so hungry. This had better be it, or you've had it. I'm so hungry I could eat every one of you—bones and all. (*He suddenly sees the Runcible Spoon*) Ahhhh! The Spoon. (*He starts to go away*) Wait a minute. (*He stops*) The silly old frump's conked out, ha, ha. With her out of the way there's nobody left I'm scared of. I can be master of the island, eat everyone and never be hungry again. Shall I eat the Spoon first? Shall I? (*He starts towards her, then stops*) No. Who wants to eat a scraggy old spinster like that? Far too tough—give me indigestion. (*He licks his lips again*) But I am hungry—she'd be all right boiled in oil to make her tender. Yes, why not? (*He advances towards her menacingly*)
Pussycat (*as the Plum Pudding Flea gets close to the Runcible Spoon*) Fire, everybody fire.

With whoops and shouts, they all start throwing coins at the Plum Pudding Flea. To do this Owl and Pussycat come in front of the Bong Tree

Plum Pudding Flea (*taken by surprise and driven back*) Ahhhh! Help! You rotters. Mind my spots, you're hurting my spots—ow—oo—beasts—(*etc.*)

One by one they run out of ammunition, until Pussycat throws the last coin

Pussycat (*to Owl*) What can we do, that's all the money gone, and he's still there.

Plum Pudding Flea (*opening his eyes and looking round*) Aha. They've stopped. No more ammo, I'll be bound. (*To Owl and Pussycat*) Right, you'll pay for this.

Owl Oh, Pussy, this is it.

Dong Help.

All begin to make frightened noises

Plum Pudding Flea Here I come.

The Plum Pudding Flea starts hopping towards Owl and Pussycat. The screams grow louder and louder

> *In the nick of time, Professor Bosh and the Quangle Wangle enter along the back rostrum. Professor Bosh carries his net*

Quangle Wangle There he is!

They stealthily but quickly advance down the central rostrum. They net the Plum Pudding Flea just as he reaches Owl and Pussycat.
  Cheers of joy, congratulations, etc., during which the Quangle Wangle goes to the Runcible Spoon and tries to revive her. The others group round the Professor. - Stand in front of hiding places.

Owl Well done, Professor, you've saved us all.

Professor Bosh Not at all. Delighted to be of assistance, old man. Come along, you saucy specimen—we're off now.

Plum Pudding Flea Oh, don't eat me, please—I'm poisonous and horridible.

Professor Bosh I know. I don't want to eat you. We're off to my private zoo. You'll be my prize exhibit and I'll feed you on plum pudding and jam.

Plum Pudding Flea But I don't like plum pudding and I hate jam. (*He wails*)

Professor Bosh Farewell, Dong. Many thanks for your admirable assistance. Look after your Jumbly Girl. Good-bye, all.

Everyone waves and shouts good-bye

> *Professor Bosh exits, dragging the Plum Pudding Flea in the net behind him. The Turkey enters along the back rostrum, and down the central rostrum, brandishing a pistol*

Turkey Where is he? Where is he? I'll get that pea with my flistol.

All duck as the Turkey brandishes the pistol in all directions. The Runcible Spoon is still recovering

Quangle Wangle You're too late. You've got to be quicker, Vicar. (*To the Runcible Spoon*) Oh, come along, Spoon.

The Runcible Spoon stands and is looked after by the Turkey and Jumbly 2. Owl, Pussycat and the Quangle Wangle stand a pace or two in front of the main group

Pussycat Thank you, Quangle.
Quangle Wangle Don't thank me. The Professor did it.
Pussycat I know. But thank you for our exciting journey.
Owl Yes, we wouldn't be married if you hadn't helped us.
Quangle Wangle (*stepping forward and taking in the whole audience*) Well, you know, any time you want accommodation, all of which is glorious, galloobrious and genteel, at prices ranging from the reasonable to the ridiculous, don't forget to visit the Quangle Wangle's Hat Hotel. And now it's time for celebrations, wedding ones and victory over the Plum Pudding Flea ones. And here's to a happy future—for everyone.

Music. All take their positions for the final song. The sun flies out and the moon flies in

No. 15   SONG: BY THE LIGHT OF THE MOON

All A meloobious sound
Echoes over the sands;
The sight of the stars
Lifts our hearts and our hands,
As we dance by the light of the moon.

Nippity nee
Tilly loo;
You love me,
I love you.
Nippity nee
Tilly loo;
Now all change your partners,
Say how do you do?

And the walloping waves
Even wallop in time,
The wind through the Bong Trees
Is blowing a rhyme,
As we dance by the light of the moon.

Nippity nee
Tilly loo;
You love me,
I love you.
Nippity nee
Tilly loo;
Now all change your partners,
Say how do you do.

Nippity nee
Tilly loo;
You love me,
I love you.
Nippity nee
Tilly loo;
Good luck, Owl and Pussy,
And good luck to you.
And good luck to you.

All turn upstage as the lighting changes for a final silhouette against the cyclorama

The Plum Pudding Flea is led by Professor Bosh across the back rostrum as the others wave good-bye

CURTAIN

SET AND PROPERTY LIST

ACT I

SCENE 1

On stage: 2 flown "rope" Bong trees, folded up
        stile c of back rostrum

Off stage: boat
        guitar inside boat
        honey-pot; inside it a piece of material to represent honey
        four bags of money
        five-pound note

Personal: **Owl:** handkerchief
        Pussycat: handkerchief

SCENE 3

Strike: Stile

On stage: crumpetty tree flown in
        flat bong trees on
        sun flown in

Off stage: Quangle Wangle's hat
        honey-pot, bags of money inside the five-pound note

Personal: **Runcible Spoon:** spectacles, smelling salts, Victorian dolly bag
        Professor Bosh: huge net, card, magnifying glass on a string, umbrella
          strapped on the back, notebook and pencil on a string, pocket-
          book, mallet, stethoscope round the neck

SCENE 4

Strike: flat Bong tree

SCENE 5

Off stage: honey-pot, bags of money inside the five-pound note
        boulders

Personal: **Professor Bosh:** as before, except for net
        Dong: net

SCENE 6

Off stage: Bags of money inside the five-pound note (Owl)

Personal: Pig: ring

ACT II

SCENE 1

On stage: flat Bong tree

Off stage: sieve
"honey"

Personal: **Head Jumbly:** scroll
Professor Bosh: as before, plus card made of rice paper

SCENE 2

Strike: flat Bong tree

Off stage: bags of money inside the five-pound note (**Quangle Wangle**)

SCENE 3

On stage: Turkey's house, 2 flat Bong trees, barrel

Off stage: bags of money inside five-pound note (**Quangle Wangle**)
Prayer Book (**Turkey**)
buttonhole (**Quangle Wangle**)
bouquet (**Runcible Spoon**)
truncheon (**Turkey**)

Off stage: table for cookery scene; wedding cake ready inside
(waiting to be brought on during the "wedding feast" song):
colander
bowl
squeezy-type sauce container
2 brooms
soup ladle
saucepan
2 dog bones
tin of nuts
tin of bolts
oil can
cookery book; spring snake inside
2 strips of beef
1 egg in a basket
specimen box (for snake)

SCENE 4

Strike: cookery scene props (**Jumblies**) at the end of scene

---

SCENE 5

Strike: Turkey's house, revealing behind 2 tables of food on the central
             rostrum; and 9 goblets

Off stage: pistol (**Turkey**)
             net (**Professor Bosh**)

ACT I

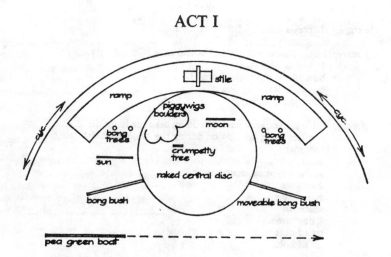

ACT II

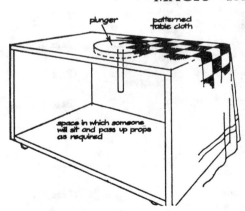

cyc → ramp ramp ← *cyc*

moon

° bong °
trees

° bong °
trees

sun

bong bush

barrel

turkeys/
cottage

bong bush

jumblies
sleeve

"MAGIC" TABLE

plunger   patterned
           table cloth

space in which someone
will sit and pass up props
as required

The table is boxed in on three sides. The floor is on castors. A person is able to sit inside this space, and by removing the plunger is able to hand up or receive props as required. The props are set beside him/her, e.g. wedding cake, etc.

The plunger is simply cut out of the table top and covered in the same fabric as the table so that when it is in position the audience cannot tell that a hole is there. By using a patterned fabric, i.e. large checks, or flowers, the small crack between the plunger and the table does not show.

LIGHTING PLOT

Property fittings required: nil

One basic setting throughout

ACT I

To open: Effect of mysterious semi-darkness

EFFECTS PLOT

ACT I

ACT II

MADE AND PRINTED IN GREAT BRITAIN BY
LATIMER TREND & COMPANY LTD PLYMOUTH